Sergeei Mikhailovich Kravchinskii

King Stork and King Log

Sergeei Mikhailovich Kravchinskii
King Stork and King Log
ISBN/EAN: 9783743407701
Manufactured in Europe, USA, Canada, Australia, Japa
Cover: Foto ©ninafisch / pixelio.de

Manufactured and distributed by brebook publishing software (www.brebook.com)

Sergeei Mikhailovich Kravchinskii

King Stork and King Log

KING STORK AND KING LOG. *A Study of Modern Russia.* By STEPNIAK

IN TWO VOLUMES
VOL. II.

DOWNEY & CO., 12 YORK STREET, COVENT GARDEN, LONDON, 1895. [*All rights reserved*]

KING STORK AND KING LOG:

A STUDY OF MODERN RUSSIA.

EDUCATED RUSSIA UNDER ALEXANDER III.

I.

THE opposition in Russia has always been chiefly stimulated by sympathy for the downtrodden masses. If autocracy could make the peasants prosperous and contented, this would be an infallible means for preventing revolution. The feeling of personal independence is weak in Russia, compared with that engrossing pity and love for the masses into which all our social instincts seem absorbed.

But the bureaucratic despotism cannot benefit the masses. Despotism implies suppression of individual initiative, educational restrictions, obstacles to any concerted action, and general lawlessness, which must all prove most baleful to the class that has no means of self-defence. The peasants have fared very badly under Alexander III., as we have just seen; and the worse their position, the more favourable the soil for revolutionary agitation.

Judging by the evidence of facts, we must admit that the Government was conscious of this close relation between its sins against the masses and the danger of retribution.

Although there were no terrorist attempts to provoke reprisals, we notice through all the reign of Alexander III. a constant increase of precaution against his enemies. The system of administrative punishments, directed, as it is well known, against those who are merely suspected of being likely some day to become political offenders — this iniquitous system received a new development. Until then, exile to distant provinces, including the inhabitable part of Siberia, had been considered sufficient to protect the throne from the attacks of young people—students of both sexes who were only just legally of age. Alexander III. did not feel secure on these terms. An important aggravation was introduced in the form of *imprisonment by administrative order*, i.e. without any form of trial, without any proper examination of the accused, who often do not know either the names of their accusers, nor the exact nature of the charges which have been brought against them.

In the Wyborg district of St. Petersburg there is a prison, which is called colloquially "The Cross," on account of its shape. But it is not by the shape alone that it deserves to be named after the emblem of suffering. There is no worse prison in the Empire. The isolation is complete, the confinement strictly solitary, with hard labour, and prohibition of books, except those which the Government lends the prisoners. There is no communication with the outer world.

In the autumn of 1887 "The Cross" began to be populated with administrative prisoners. In the beginning of 1888 "The Cross" had already twenty-five inmates; soon it vied with the House of Preventative Detention, of Shpalerny Street, the number of administrative prisoners immured there being already over a hundred, and now the prison is filled to its full capacity.

This is an altogether new departure in the efforts of the Government to stamp out opposition. The terms of imprisonment which may be thus inflicted arbitrarily are fixed at three years, a terribly long term, for Russians in particular, who, with their nervous organization, cannot support, as Galkin Vrassky admits, more than six months of solitary confinement.

The experiment is new, and up to the present the terms of imprisonment inflicted by the administration are in most cases short—varying from six months to sixteen. It is rarely over two years. But *l'appetit vient en mangeant!* In less than five years this first hesitation has been got over, and the term of imprisonment by administrative order has been increased to ten years.

In the meantime, let me tell the reader the story of one of its first inmates, a girl condemned to what was then the longest term— two and a half years—whose case will serve as a sample for the rest, and will throw some light upon certain practices of the Russian police.

In 1888, a certain Bychkov, a Siberian exile, escaped from his place of banishment and arrived at Moscow in the autumn of the same year. He had little money, no passport, and no acquaintances in the town. In this extremity he went into a small coffee-room near the University, and, after having observed for some time the people who were there, he fixed upon a girl, a perfect stranger to him, whom he followed in the street when she left the coffee-room. Here he approached her, and told her who he was and what was his position. The girl proved to be Alexandra Kopylova, a student of liberal views. She believed Bychkov's story, and promised to do what she could for him. But she could not do much. In October Bychkov was re-arrested by the police, who made a domiciliary visit at the rooms of Kopylova as well. Nothing compromising was discovered, except one copy of a Geneva revolutionary (Radical) paper, called *Self-Government*. She was, as a matter of course, imprisoned. But the police had nothing particular to be proud of. Bychkov himself was not a very great prize, for he was a simple exile, who had nothing more important against him than a slight connection with peaceful propaganda among the St. Petersburg workmen. The police resolved to utilize him in another way. After a long interrogation, Bychkov was taken to the district prison (*chast*); but here it somehow occurred that all the cells were full, and there was no room for the new inmate. The officer of gendarmerie declared himself much displeased, but agreed to the director's proposal to lock up the prisoner for the night in a room in the fire tower. It thus happened that Bychkov was confined in an ordinary room with a window looking upon the street. It was rather high, but it was near the water-pipe running along the wall outside, and there was 'a slanting roof of the lower storey which could be utilized for the descent. The prisoner could not lose such an opportunity, and in the dead of the night, when he thought the house plunged in sleep, he opened the window and descended into the street, congratulating himself upon a happy escape.

But his position was still a very precarious one, for he had to find a hiding-place at once, and that was not easy at such a time. He thought of a man of good position, a Liberal, a Professor of the Moscow University, whom he had met once at Kopylova's room, and he went to knock at his door. He was recognized, told his story, and was admitted into the house.

This is precisely what the police expected, for the whole affair was arranged on purpose, and Bychkov was followed from the prison to the house where he found refuge. But he could not stay for long at the same house, and changed his hiding-place several times during the few days the police allowed him to roam about the town.

Of course all his movements were closely watched. When he was arrested, all those who had given him a temporary refuge were arrested likewise. Golzev, Nikolaev, and Sokolov were of their number—all men of good social position, professors, editors of influential papers, members of the Moscow Town Council. All were put in prison—Sokolov together with his wife. To the latter, unprepared as she was for this rather uncommon experience, the shock was so great that she lost her reason after two months of solitary confinement. The others were released after a few months detention. As to Miss Alexandra Kopylova, who was the "principal" offender in the great crime of harbouring an administrative exile escaping from his place of banishment, she had to undergo a year and a half of preliminary detention, and then was condemned, without trial, by administrative order, to two and a half years of imprisonment in "The Cross."

"The Cross" is not the only place where administrative prisoners are immured.

In 1881 the "House of Terror," the Kharkov central prison, where the early propagandists were being slowly killed, was abolished in order to appease Russian public opinion, which was roused by the tales of the horrors which went on there. Its inmates were transferred in a body to the Kara prison.

Now the Kharkov central prison is once again reopened, this time for *administrative* prisoners.

The husband of the unfortunate Nadejda Sihida, flogged to death at Kara in November, 1889, died there in 1889. Among those who are pining there are Petrovsky, Alexandroff, and Chernov under the charge of "connection with the manufacturing of bombs," though the "connection" is very distant; in fact, they are merely guilty of not having turned informers at the first favourable opportunity. One of them *saw* where Orjikh was hiding three dynamite bombs. Another, Chernov, a man of position, and not a revolutionist at all, is imprisoned because a revolutionist, who expected to be arrested in the street, left two bombs in his house *without Chernov's knowledge*. When he discovered what the dangerous parcel contained, he threw the bombs in the pond instead of going with them to the police.

As to administrative exile proper—that scourge of modern Russia—it has been terribly aggravated under Alexander III.

According to former rules the maximum of banishment which could be inflicted without trial, by a simple order of the administration, was five years. It is a long term, considering that the administration has full option of prolonging it, in case of "bad behaviour" and "impenitence."

But it seemed not enough, and the maximum has been extended to ten years, which means practically to a lifetime. Few will be able to outlive such long terms; so that the administration will be saved the trouble of repeating blow after blow upon its chosen victims: now they may be killed with one single blow.

This new measure has not passed through the stages which every new law passes in Russia. We have not even seen it promulgated by a ministerial circular, which, in Russia, has the force of law. It was enacted quietly, and revealed its existence by its practical application to several persons in 1887. Among the first to whom it was applied in full were Brajnikov and Sterenberg. Their crime was that both of them were *on very good terms with Boris Orjikh*, one of the noblest and most daring leaders of Russian revolution of these later days. Orjikh was the organiser of several conspiracies, the founder of a secret printing office and of a dynamite manufactory. He was tried, with twenty-nine of his accomplices, on November, 1888, and condemned to death. The sentence was not executed on account of mere material obstacles: the two years of preliminary detention brought Orjikh to the verge of the grave, so that he had to be carried upon a litter to the court. At that time the Government had not yet discovered that a man can be hung from his bed, as was done with Bernstein, in Yakutsk. So Orjikh was sent to Schlusselbourg, where he died a few months later. As to Brajnikoff and Sterenberg, they were not tried, for the very simple reason that there was no proof whatever of their guilt. There was only *suspicion* that they must have *known* something about Orjikh's doings, and must have been in sympathy with his views, since they were his intimate friends—a very common charge in Russia, for which formerly people were punished at the utmost by five years of exile. The prolongation of the maximum means simply a general aggravation of penalties inflicted by administrative order.

Those who formerly were visited with five years of banishment will now have ten, and those who had two and a half will have five. The examination of other cases of the infliction of the maximum terms of exile leave no room for doubt of this.

The Government seems to grudge the old exiles the shortness of the penalties, inflicted under former regulations, and has introduced some new methods of remedying the evil. As we have mentioned above, it was always in the power of the administration to prolong the term of exile for " bad conduct," which means for some attempt on the part of the exile to protect himself against the coarse and brutal administration. But since 1883 we come across a number of cases where the exile has in no way provoked the displeasure of the local autocrats, and yet had had his penalty aggravated in consequence of the *re-examination* (sometimes many years after) *of old documents*, upon which the administration has already given a decision.

This is a new proceeding, and however trifling, as compared with the total mass of wrongs done by administrative exile, it is worth mentioning, for it characterises the utter disrespect of the

Russian Government for human suffering and the most elementary principles of justice—we may say, of public morality.

But why, the reader will ask, should the gendarmes burden themselves with ransacking the archives of the State police, when they have so many fresh cases upon their hands?

We are told that it is done as a good exercise for the young officers of this respectable body. When a young gendarme is admitted into the political branch of the service, they do not trust him with new cases, but give him an old one for re-examination to test his ability. He has then to give an opinion upon it, and if he discovers something which tells against the exile, and has been over-looked, a few years more are added to the latter's original term of banishment.

We do not vouch for the accuracy of the *explanation*. It may be that the old cases are re-examined on some other grounds. The fact is that they *are* re-examined, and new penalties are inflicted upon the victims for no other reason. The unexpectedness of such new blows appears probably to the gendarmes in the light of a good practical joke, though for those concerned it is rarely a matter for joking, and sometimes a cause of bitter tears.

In November, 1880, Antimas Gomcralidze, an Armenian by birth, condemned in 1877 by the St. Petersburg tribunal to exile in Siberia, returned to his country after the expiration of his term. His crime was not particularly grave. In 1875-6 the police discovered in Moscow a "secret society," composed of about a dozen young men and girls, the oldest of whom was twenty-three, the youngest sixteen. Their object was the propaganda of Socialist ideas among workmen. They were all condemned to various punishments, Gomcralidze among the rest. Since that time for full sixteen years he had been dragged from one prison to another, from one wretched Siberian hamlet to another. His health was ruined, his strength broken. From a blooming youth of twenty-two, as he was at the time of the trial, he became a grey-haired, decrepit old man.

But he was in his country once again. The long years of trial were forgotten. He began to feel his strength renewed in his home. But he had not much time to enjoy his freedom. Before five months elapsed, in April, 1889, a large body of police came, and the officer told him that he was to be once again sent to Siberia. He was arrested, and without any explanation taken to the Kutais prison.

The neighbours, for the most part small farmers and peasants, whom he had befriended as a physician, collected a sum of money, and sent a man to Kutais to make inquiries, and intercede if possible with the governor in favour of Gomcralidze. The man went, and succeeded in interesting in the fate of his client several persons of good position in the town. They spoke to the governor of the province, and to the local gendarme officer, who all seemed disposed in favour of the hapless man. Indeed, Gomcralidze could not possibly be of any danger to the "throne and the existing institutions" in the out-of-the-way corner where he had settled. The village where he lived was ninety miles away from Kutais, and sixty miles from the postal highway, so that he was as much isolated there as he would be in the Narym marshes, whither he was to be re-exiled. The only difference was that of a better climate, which was so necessary to his broken health. But the local authorities could do nothing for him. The order for re-arresting and exiling him came from St. Petersburg, and the reason was as follows :—

A STUDY OF MODERN RUSSIA. 15

Three years before, whilst Gomcralidze was living in Tomsk, the pupils of the gymnasium (grammar school) had founded a small library of their own for their personal edification. It consisted only of books authorized by the Russian censorship. Not a single revolutionary pamphlet had been found there, or seen circulated among the pupils. Still, the small library contained works like Thomas Buckle's "History of Civilization in England," and some of Herbert Spencer's. This showed that the boys were of a serious and rather progressive turn of mind. Still, the affair would have been probably hushed up if the discovery of the library had not coincided with the attempt upon the Tzar, Alexander III., which occurred in St. Petersburg on the 13th of March, 1887.

Panic-stricken, the superintendents of the Tomsk grammar school looked upon the harmless affair as a sort of political crime. A number of boys were thrown into prison on the charge of conspiracy and secret propaganda, and ordered, under the threat of heavy punishment to confess everything, which meant to betray those who gave them books or money to buy them, or encouraged them in any other way. Gomcralidze knew nothing about this library.

But in his quality of surgeon's assistant he paid occasional visits to the house of one of the boys who contributed a certain number of books to the common library. Being arrested, the boy named Gomeralidze as the person who gave him these books, on the childish consideration that since he was already a political offender and an exile, it would not matter for him.

The charge was not supported by facts, and the boy himself retracted it afterwards. Gomeralidze was summoned to the police office, but his explanations satisfied the local authorities, so that he was not molested, and when his term of banishment ended he was allowed, as we have seen, to return to his native country.

But in this interval the famous General Rusinov—the man who is mentioned by Mr. George Kennan in the *Century* in connection with the obliteration of the inscriptions upon the exiles' tombstones, and the would-be discovery of a secret printing press in Yakutsk— this General Rusinov visited Tomsk on the pretext of inquiring into the condition of the exiles—in reality in order to report upon their conduct.

Together with other materials, he brought with him to St. Petersburg the documents referring to Gomcralidze's offence. Here it was given for revision to a young pushing officer of gendarmerie, who discovered, as he thought, some hints throwing doubts upon the correctness of Gomcralidze's former acquittal by the Tomsk gendarmes; and without any verification, without examination of the accused, an order for his re-exile for another three years was despatched to Kutais.

In 1893 Gomcralidze was allowed to return to his native place, on the expiration of his new term. But his health was ruined past recovery, and he died a few months after his return to Kutais.

The case is not unique. In 1878 a St. Petersburg student, Tutcheff, was arrested, and condemned, without trial, by administrative order, to five years' banishment in the Yakutsk region. His term expired in 1883, and his family expected him home. But he did not come, and in his stead a letter arrived informing the parents that his term of banishment was prolonged.

Then his father, a general in the Tzar's army, went to the officer of the State police to inquire what new offence his son had committed to have merited a new punishment. In consideration of his official position he was received, and an explanation vouchsafed to him by the gendarmerie, and it was this: his son had committed no new offence, but they had re-examined the old document referring to his case, and, finding that the original punishment was inadequate, had added on for young Tutcheff another two years of banishment.

We will mention, as a further illustration of this curious practice, the case of Sineff, a private of one of the regiments of guards, exiled to Urjum in 1886; the police having discovered that he paid occasional visits to the former schoolmaster of his village, who proved to be implicated in some conspiracies. Sineff's term of banishment expired in November, 1888, but, instead of being allowed to return to his home, he was ordered to remain at his place of punishment indefinitely, "pending the re-examination of his case."

In 1887, an exile named Peshekherov, after having completed his three years' term of banishment in Ust Kamenogorsk (Semipalatinsk region), was returning with his wife and children to European Russia by permission of the local authorities, and had already reached Tomsk, which stands about 600 miles from Ust Kamenogorsk, when suddenly a telegram came from St. Petersburg inflicting upon him another two years of exile.

The Siberian authorities were as much surprised at this order as Peshekherov himself, as there was never any conflict between him and the administration during the three years of his involuntary residence at Ust Kamenogorsk.

In 1884 a student, Raspopin, accused of "militarism," which means *holding the opinion* that the Revolutionists ought, for the good of their cause, to get as many commissions as possible in the army, was exiled for two years to Beresov, one of the most awful of Siberian penitentiary towns, situated in the marshes of the Arctic zone. Still, the term of his punishment was a short one. But at its expiration in 1886 two more years were added to it after re-examination of his case. But it seems that the documents concerning Raspopin were either written in very good handwriting or put in a very conspicuous place, or offered some peculiar attraction, as certain problems in chess. The fact is that, after the expiration of his additional term in 1888, his case was re-examined once again, and another year was added to his term. This was a small addition, a mere trifle, according to the gendarmes' views; but Raspopin seems not to have duly appreciated their leniency, for he died in Beresov a few months later from scurvy, which he had contracted there.

Bogorodzky, the son of the commander of the fortress of SS. Peter and Paul, who was exiled in 1883 to Tunka for his revolutionary sympathies; Martynov, a well-known physician; Ivanchin Pisarev, a journalist, and a score of others, have been made the victims of this exercise of the gendarmes' wits—receiving unexpectedly and unwarrantably, some two, some three or more additional years of punishment, just when they were packing their things for the journey home. A cruel joke, telling not only upon its victims, but upon the whole mass of exiles; adding to that sense of the absolute insecurity of the future, which is one of the most grievous aspects of the life of exiles.

II.

IN the regulations referring to the exile system there is no restriction as to the place to which the administration can send a man, woman, or child whom they consider a danger to the security of the Tzar. But it was originally taken for granted that the place of exile should be more or less habitable for civilized beings. Taking into account the circumstances under which this penalty was inflicted, it cannot be said that such a restriction erred on the side of leniency. But under Alexander III. it was entirely thrown aside, and the practice of exiling people to places utterly unfit for human habitation was introduced on a large scale. This has made exile sometimes a heavier penalty than penal servitude in the Siberian mines.

Siberia is a vast country, with many climates, many gaols, many towns, which are all places of punishment.

The climate of Southern Siberia is as good as

that of Central Russia, even better sometimes. The towns of Irkutsk, Tobolsk, Krasnoyarsk, and several others, resemble in all respects ordinary provincial towns of European Russia. The Siberian people are a clever, industrious race, who never have known serfdom, and are now rapidly growing in education and prosperity. The thirst for knowledge is pervading all the well-to-do classes; and such is the scarcity of people who have received a good education that a professional man of any kind is sure to find a permanent and remunerative employment.

The exiles are mostly well educated men and women, often professional people. They could easily make a living in the larger towns, and protect themselves from want even in the smaller ones, numbering only a few thousand inhabitants. But here we stumble against the monstrous ministerial regulation of March, 1881, forbidding the political exiles to give lessons, to practise as doctors, advocates, lawyers, photographers, printers, librarians, booksellers, &c.,—indeed, to do anything which is likely to bring them in contact with the surrounding population.

But this regulation is not always rigorously enforced. The earnings of wives who have voluntarily followed their exiled husbands, and are not subjected to these restrictions; the money received by some of the well-to-do exiles from their relatives at home ; and, above all, the spirit of fellowship prevailing among the exiles, who live generally in small communes of three, five, or more persons, rich and poor together, sharing all in a truly fraternal way—all this accounts for the fact that in the larger towns the exiles suffer no very great material want. Here they have to bear moral sufferings due to their absolute dependence upon the caprice of a brutal, ignorant administration, which intercepts their private letters, seizes books, makes domiciliary searches at any time of day and night, deprives them whenever it chooses of their means of livelihood, and re-exiles them to worse places at will. The collisions between the exiles and the administration, of which we hear now and then, are all due to these causes.

The system of administrative exile is one of the heaviest charges against our Government. The incalculable harm done to Russia by its practice on so vast a scale, consists in the intellectual stultification of thousands of really well-intentioned, honest, and patriotic men and women, whose services would be invaluable to the country.

George Kennan has described to the indignant world our exile system as a whole. I will not retrace his steps in speaking of that national calamity of ours. My object is to say a few words about the exile into the Far North not visited by Kennan, where the exiles have to undergo not merely complete intellectual isolation, but a series of most cruel physical and material sufferings, which make that form of arbitrary punishment just as heavy as, if not heavier than, the hard labour in the mines.

Let me tell the reader the story of one of the early settlers in that inhospitable region, a certain Zalessky, a land surveyor in the province of Kursk. In 1877 he was arrested on the charge of having distributed a few Socialist pamphlets, and exiled without trial to Verkoyansk, a village at a latitude of 67° 34', numbering 290 inhabitants, wretchedly poor, and completely savage. In that awful place, where he was at that time the only educated man, Zalessky remained *for full eight years*, without a book, without a newspaper, without a letter, suffering from the terrible Arctic cold, from hunger, and want. It was not the cruelty of the gendarmes which inflicted so dire a punishment for so trifling an offence, it was their carelessness.

Zalessky was simply *forgotten* by them. When, by mere accident, his existence was discovered, an order was sent to Siberia to bring him back to his native country. As he had no money to make the journey at his own expense, he had to travel right across Siberia on foot, under escort, with a batch of vagabonds sent to their native villages in European Russia. It took him a year to come to the Moscow central prison, which he reached in 1886: there he was met by a number of political exiles on their way to Siberia. One of them, who escaped aftewards, told me that the appearance of Zalessky was that of a man who had spent twenty years in a gloomy dungeon. Though under forty, he looked like an old decrepit man, with bent and shattered body, blinking, almost sightless eyes, toothless mouth.

It is not only the climate which works such havoc with a man's frame, but the life of utter misery and isolation. Whenever an exile is sent to a new place, where he is quite alone, his fate is always extremely hard. Here is another example of more recent date. In 1884 Jordan, a student of the Kharkov Veterinary Schools, was arrested for having taken part in the printing of the pamphlets of the *peaceful* Socialists—

those who were against political terrorism. After a year of imprisonment, namely in 1885, he was exiled without trial to Verkolensk (not Verkhoyansk), a town in Southern Siberia. On reaching this place he wrote to his friends at Kharkov asking them to send him at his own address all the new things issued by the secret press, saying that the local police superintendent was a good man, who did not open the letters of the exiles. This letter was intercepted by the Kharkov police, and Jordan was sent off to the Arctic zone to Vilusk, lat. 63° 45', where he had to live quite alone among the savage Yakuts. The sufferings and privations he had to undergo were such that he died there in 1888.

The case of Miss Lidia Ananyn, a young delicate girl of sixteen, who had nothing to do with revolutions, is also a very hard one, though it did not end so tragically. Her story shows the proceedings of the Russian police when the "highest of all," which means the Tzar, is personally concerned.

In March, 1887, there was an unsuccessful attempt against the life of the present Tzar, which was not exactly an attempt, because the conspirators were arrested beforehand. One of them, Novorussky, executed afterwards, lodged in the house of Mrs. Ananyn, a widow of forty-two, with two children—a girl, Lidia, and a boy, Nicolas, to whom Novorussky gave lessons. It was proved that Novorussky made bombs in his room with a fellow-conspirator; but there was no evidence whatever that his landlady knew or suspected anything about it. Indeed, she did not, having her business as midwife of the Municipal Hospital to attend to. Yet she was sentenced by the military tribunal to hard labour and sent to Kara. Her son, a boy of thirteen, because he was a pupil of so dangerous a man as Novorussky, was exiled to the Caucasus. The daughter, Lidia, simply because she was three years older, met with a heavier punishment. She was exiled to the village Kandinsky, near Beresov, a horrible place, lat. 67°, where she was thrown quite alone among the savages. She petitioned to be sent to Kara, to be near her mother; but this was refused. She petitioned that her brother exiled to the Caucasus should be allowed to join her. But this was refused too. She was quite alone, suffering from cold, hunger, and all kinds of privations, which, in a little more than a year, brought her to the verge of death. She would have certainly died if by chance another exile, an energetic man with a large family, had not been sent to join her.

When the number of exiles increases, they mutually help each other morally and materially, so as to make the life more tolerable even in places so cursed by nature as Verkhoyansk, Sredne Kolymsk, and Vilusk. Still the sufferings and privations to which they are permanently subjected are extremely severe. These are uninhabitable places, for Europeans at all events. Nova Zemla, which is visited by men only during the summer months, has a much milder climate than the Arctic region of Siberia. In the former the average temperature for a year is 13° F., with 7° below zero for the three winter months, whilst in Verkhoyansk the average both for the winter and autumn months is 31° F. below zero, the average temperature for the three months of eternal night, December, January and February, sinking to 53° F. below zero, which is full 13° below the freezing point of mercury. As to the average temperature for the year, it is only 1° F. above zero, the lowest temperature that has been observed at any point of the northern hemisphere. During the short summer the temperature rises, rapidly reaching 56° F. But with the warm season come the mosquitoes, which are a plague of these regions more difficult to endure than cold. "I never would have believed," says the correspondent of the *Russky Vedomosty* (Moscow), who has been exiled to these parts, "that the insects could appear in such swarms. They literally darken the light, filling the air with an incessant noise, covering, as with a dark mantle, our horses, whose flanks were soon bleeding all over. Maddened with pain, the horses kicked and reared, but seeing that all was unavailing, they drooped their heads and submitted to the inevitable. In vain we tried to protect ourselves with veils, travelling, notwithstanding the hot weather, in winter gloves and overcoats. The mosquitoes penetrated through the sleeves under the shirts, stinging the breast and the body, which ached as if burned with fire. The more we struggled to get rid of our tormentors, the more we opened the way to new thousands of them. On arriving at the huts of the Yakuts we kindled a great fire, which made such a smoke that it pricked the eyes and choked the breath, though we lay stretched on the earthen floor. The mosquitoes disappeared, but as soon as the smoke dispersed a little, new swarms penetrated into the hut, covering all of us thickly." Such is nature in these regions. Now, what are the inhabitants, and their means of protecting themselves from its rigour?

We will quote from the same authority a few lines describing the largest of these northern settlements, Sredne Kolymsk, a "town" numbering fully 560 inhabitants. Most of them are of Russian extraction; but being for many generations isolated from all the world, and feeding exclusively on fish, they have lost the energy, industry, and versatility of Russian peasants. They are apathetic, lazy, and dull. It is considered a great sign of cleverness in a boy if he succeeds in learning to read and write in the course of eight to nine years. They know no trade, no industry, except fishing and occasionally hunting. The houses they live in can hardly be called houses, for they are badly-fitting wooden sheds *with no chimneys*, because the inhabitants do not know the use of bricks. The houses are warmed with a fire lit in the middle upon the earthen floor, the smoke passing out through a big hole in the pointed roof. It is not surprising that such houses during the winter are "infernally cold," to use the expression of our author.

Nothing grows, nothing can be got in these

regions. Everything is imported from enormous distances, and is, therefore, exceedingly dear. Bread is sold at famine prices. Candles, soap, cotton wares, matches, are fabulously dear. "In such conditions of the market," philosophically observes our author, "one has naturally to give up bread, sugar, and the many other commodities we are accustomed to consider as indispensable to a civilized man. But fish, reindeer meat, fat, and wood for burning can be obtained."

It is hardly necessary to say that there is nothing in a place like that to satisfy the intellectual cravings of a civilized man, which have also to be "given up" as a matter of course. Suffice it to mention that the letters from Russia take *six months* to come to Sredne Kolymsk. Thus the news received, and the papers—supposing the exiles have money to spare for subscribing to any—are always six months old, and the post comes only three times a year.

There is little difference between the three Arctic towns to which exiles are sent. If anything, Sredne Kolymsk is the best of them, numbering a population equal to that of the two others put together, and comparatively better off. Of Vilusk we read that its inhabitants are so poor that they gave up keeping dogs, being unable to feed them.

Now let us see for what crimes scores of young, intelligent, well-educated people are exiled to these horrible places. First of all, it must be remembered that—with a few exceptions we will mention later on—they are all administrative exiles, people who have never been tried at all, and never convicted of any offence. They have been exiled by order of the police, on suspicion that they held dangerous *opinions*, and are likely some day to commit some offence. What *grounds for a similar suspicion* are considered sufficient by the Russian Government for exiling people to such awful places we shall see best by a few examples. We take them all from one place, Sredne Kolymsk, in order to be nearer the average.

Let us begin with Isaac Sklovsky, a journalist of Jewist extraction. He was a man of position—the editor of the *Elisavergrad Leaflet*, a popular provincial paper. The charge against him is this: having made the acquaintance of an Odessa revolutionist named Dudin, who afterwards turned informer, he purchased from him two pamphlets, issued by the secret printing office, for the sum of thirty kopecks, which makes about 8*d*. in English coin. When a domiciliary search was made at Sklovsky's house, the pamphlets were *not* found. But he did not deny having purchased them, and refused to disclose what he had done with them. For this offence he was kept in prison about a year, and then released on bail at the beginning of 1885, pending the resolution upon his case. In the summer of 1886 the resolution came, and he was arrested again and marched off straight to Eastern Siberia for five years. *Because a Jew* he was sent to Sredne Kolymsk.

The case of another young Jew, Liadoff, of Riga, is still more remarkable. The reader may remember that some time ago some notice was taken by the English press of the arrest at Riga of a German sailor who brought upon an English ship a parcel of revolutionary prints. It was this fact that brought poor Liadoff into trouble. He had a prosperous business in Riga, and never thought of politics or revolution, when, one fine morning, he received from an unknown gentleman (the German sailor) a note requesting him to come on board a certain ship then in Riga harbour. Prompted by curiosity, Liadoff came and asked for the sailor. When they were alone the latter told him that he was in great difficulty: he had a parcel of revolutionary pamphlets entrusted to him by a Geneva friend, but could not find the person to whom they had to be delivered at Riga. Not knowing what to do with his dangerous parcel, he wanted to know whether Liadoff would not be good enough to take care of it. Naturally, Liadoff declined, energetically saying that he had nothing to do with revolution, and expressed his amazement how the idea of applying to him could have entered the sailor's head. The latter apologized, and explained that he got Liadoff's name from his Geneva friend, who happened to have been Liadoff's schoolfellow, and thought he might be tried if he was still in Riga. The affair did not go farther. Liadoff went home without having taken one copy of the pamphlets. But when the sailor was arrested, Liadoff's visit on board the ship was discovered by the detectives, and he had to answer for it to the police. He explained candidly how the thing passed, and was released. This took place in October, 1884. Soon after he married, and was enjoying his honeymoon, when, in January, 1887, whilst he was at dinner with his young wife, a messenger came from the colonel of gendarmerie, asking him to come immediately to his office. Liadoff was on good terms with the colonel. The office was in the same street, a few blocks off. Nothing suspecting, he left the table immediately—"just between the second course and the pudding," as he said afterwards to his companions—and went to the colonel. Here he was told that, according to a telegram from St. Petersburg, he was to be sent off to Oriental Siberia by the next train, which meant in two hours' time. It is easy to imagine the poor man's consternation. To his vehement protests and inquiries the colonel answered that he was himself exceedingly surprised at such an order, for which he was quite unable to find any plausible explanation. Liadoff begged for a respite, suggesting that there must be some error or misunderstanding. The colonel said that the order was a peremptory one, but he would grant a respite if the governor of the province authorized it. The governor, who also knew Liadoff, was applied to, and fully entered into his position. He telegraphed to St. Petersburg, vouching for Liadoff's innocence, and asking whether it was not somebody else who had to be sent to Oriental Siberia. The result was an angry telegram from St. Petersburg saying that they "do not make mistakes," and reprimanding the governor for having delayed the execution of the order. Thus, after a respite of two days only, Liadoff was marched off to Oriental Siberia. *As a Jew* he was also sent to Sredne Kolymsk.

The case of two boys sent to the same dreadful place, Landa and Gornstein, also Jews —who, when arrested, were the first fifteen, the second sixteen years of age—is more shocking still. They were both studying in the Odessa gymnasium, when, in the beginning of August, 1885, a certain Fedorsher arrived in the town from Geneva. He had been slightly compromised in some early propaganda business before he left Russia, so that on returning he had to be careful to keep out of the reach of the police. As the latter got wind of his arrival in Odessa he had to hide himself for some time in the houses of his friends, as is often the case with "illegal" people. One of these friends, being not sure that his own house was not watched by the police, had the unfortunate idea of taking Fedorsher one night to the lodgings of the two boys, who were his relatives, as the safest refuge. Of course the boys asked no questions, and were satisfied with the explanation that their guest wanted simply a lodging for a night or two to avoid the expense of an hotel. Nobody thought of the possibility of the police coming to seek Fedorsher in the house of these children. But the police came on account of the boys themselves. It was rumoured that in their gymnasium some sort of propaganda was afloat, and in one night 120 domiciliary visits were made to the houses of different pupils in order to discover some material proof of it. One of these visits fell to the lot of Landa and Gornstein. When the police arrived, the inmates were not yet in bed, and Fedorsher, on being asked who he was, explained that he was their neighbour, living a few blocks off. They believed him, and he played the part he assumed so well that the police let him go. But when his little portmanteau, which he had to leave behind, was opened, a parcel of revolutionary publications was discovered in it. This was sufficient for the arrest of the two boys, though it was clearly proved that they knew nothing about it. They were kept in the Odessa prison, one of the worst in the empire, in solitary confinement, for about a year and a half, and then the police, without any trial, pronounced upon them the verdict of five years' exile to Oriental Siberia, as people dangerous to the existing order and implicated in revolutionary agitation. When the monstrous sentence was read to them the younger of the boys, Landa, exclaimed: "How? Am I also a revolutionist, a man dangerous to the authorities?"

At this the gendarme smiled, and answered in these very words: "No, certainly you are not. But you may become so some day."

I must not leave the reader under the impression that Jews alone are honoured in Russia with this dreadful form of punishment. There are several born Russians among the exiles of Sredne Kolymsk, but they have all somewhat heavier charges against them. One of them, Belousoff, was tried by an exceptional tribunal, it is true, but still tried, and condemned to exile for life in these gloomy regions for a distant connection with a dynamite manufacturing business; another, Victor Daniloff, though never tried, was involved in active revolutionary propaganda among the dissenting sects; the third had escaped once from Southern Siberia; the fourth was for several years the special correspondent and representative of a revolutionary paper. All these are small offences as compared with the punishment, but they are actual crimes when compared with the ridiculous charges against the Jews who share the same fate.

The anti-Semitic agitation we have seen in Germany and Austria is as absurd and ridiculous as would be the revival of some exploded superstition. But in Russia we see something worse. Here, in consequence of the personal bias of the Tzar, Alexander III., who is a fierce Jew hater, a special measure was passed in 1886, making one section of citizens liable to heavier punishments than others for the same offences, simply because they are of a certain race and creed. Is it not a crying injustice, a flagrant and cynical violation of the fundamental laws of all modern States, Russia included, where the equality of all the citizens before the Tzar or his representatives stands in the written code? We need not multiply our illustrations. The cases of Belousoff, Daniloff, and Miss Shmidova, a young girl of Jewish extraction, whose only offence is that she was the sweetheart of Ulianoff, the would-be Tzaricide, present the maximum of guilt; the cases of Liadoff and the two boys we have just spoken of, the minimum. All the rest of the thirty exiles in Sredne Kolymsk stand between.

The exiles of Verkho Yansk are in the same position as those of Sredne Kolymsk—the same offences, or rather absence of offences, the same conditions of life. We will record here only two men, who have suffered there for many years, and will probably find there their icy graves, Porfiry Voinaralsky and Sergius Kovalik. They are now both about forty-five, and must be by this time utterly broken, decrepit old men. Both were justices before being arrested: Voinaralsky in the province of Penza; Kovalik in Orel. In 1873, at the epoch of the enthusiastic crusade of educated people "among the peasants," they abandoned their magisterial chairs, and as simple manual labourers went among the people to preach Socialism. They were arrested very soon—in July, 1874. Since that time, for sixteen years, the Government has been tormenting these two men with a mean and implacable cruelty, simply because they have shown more devotion to the cause, more energy, and have won a greater popularity than the rest. They were dragged from prison to prison; from the fortress of Peter and Paul to the house of horrors, the Kharkoff central prison;

then to Kara, where they were arbitrarily kept after the term of their legal punishment had elapsed. And when they ought to have been set free to settle in some Siberian town, like many of their companions, they were exiled to Verkho Yansk, where, up to 1885, they remained alone with Zalessky, mentioned above, suffering the same horrible privations which have broken the latter. And all this life of martyrdom for a few words about Socialism!

The Government of Alexander III. showed, after 1886, a decided inclination to multiply and extend the practice of administrative exile to the Arctic zone. The towns of Sredne Kolymsk and Verkho Yansk have been populated, as we have said, within the last three years. In Vilusk, a town at the same latitude, a special prison has been constructed for the unfortunate survivors of the Yakutsk massacres of 1889—a fact which is unique in the history of penitentiary institutions. It is reported that a project is afloat of instituting a new penal colony at Bykoff promontory, which is still farther advanced in the region of eternal ice. Thus the Russian Government has created for its political suspects a sort of combination of Dante's *antenora*, described in Canto XXXII. of the *Inferno*, where the sinners are tormented by being immersed in solid ice, with the first *girone* described in Canto III., where the damned are tormented by mosquitoes and wasps.

Every government pretending to be a civilized one is morally bound to respect certain general principles of justice and equity; just as a man admitted into respectable society is bound to conform to certain rules of common decency.

The Russian Government has grossly outraged them. I need not dwell upon the difference in the treatment of Jews and Christians, which is a monstrosity. I will only ask whether the foundation of penitentiary colonies of any kind in the Arctic zone is not a monstrosity as well. Imprisonments are intended as deprivation of freedom and nothing more. Exile is intended as a limitation of the freedom of movement. To aggravate these punishments purposely by physical sufferings so intense as those caused by the Arctic climate is to reintroduce torture under another form.

I cannot leave this painful subject without drawing the attention of all humanitarian people to another shocking trait of the Siberian exile system: the treatment of men who are undoubtedly insane. Insanity is not rare among political prisoners, thanks to the whole system of our solitary confinement. Sometimes the insane are sent to the asylums, or consigned to the care of their relatives; but sometimes they are not; and we know positively of several men, undoubtedly insane, who are kept in the worst places of exile, marched with the parties of other prisoners by *étapes*, and treated as if they were as responsible as people who are right in their minds.

A certain Edelson was exiled in 1887 to Verkho Yansk, although he was undoubtedly mad. He was arrested at the close of 1885 in Minsk on the charge of participation in an unsuccessful attempt to found a secret printing office. At the preliminary interrogation, at which in Russia a prisoner is bound to answer, and which in case of political offences is conducted in the truly Jesuitic and inquisitorial manner, Edelson had the misfortune of falling into one of the traps laid for him by the gendarmes. He committed some indiscretion, making statements to the prejudice of his companions. The pain he felt at the discovery of his error was so keen that he lost his reason a few months after his imprisonment. This did not prevent the police from exiling him to the

Arctic zone. He was marched in company with twenty other political prisoners and four hundred common convicts across Siberia, causing his companions endless trouble and worry. His fixed idea was that they were conspiring to kill him, though they treated him very kindly, and have forgiven him long ago his involuntary offence so heavily expiated. Every now and then in the dead of the night he would terrify them all with wild howlings and cries, asking for the officer of the escort or the director of the prison, imploring them to protect him and separate him from his companions. So they reached Irkutsk. Here the political exiles petitioned that Edelson should be tranferred to the Irkutsk lunatic asylum. The local authorities supported that petition, telegraphing to St. Petersburg that Edelson was really insane. But no reply came, and Edelson was marched off to Verkho Yansk. How the other exiles managed with him there, God alone knows.

This is no exception. Almost in every batch of exiles marching to Siberia there are men in a similar condition. With the party that left Moscow central prison in May, 1887, there were two men undoubtedly insane. One was Tikhon Lebedeff, the scion of a wealthy family, and a well-educated man. After having completed his studies in the gymnasium, instead of going to the university, he became a common workman, and took an active part in organizing the "Workmen's League" of Southern Russia. In 1881 he was arrested at Kieff on suspicion, and confined in Nijni Novgorod. He escaped very soon, and resumed his favourite propagandist work among the workmen in Odessa, Kieff, and St. Petersburg. He was arrested in the latter town in the summer of 1884, and imprisoned in the fortress of Peter and Paul. Here he became raving mad, and was transferred to the Kazan lunatic asylum, where there is a special ward provided for politicals. He recovered his reason, and was again immured in the fortress of Peter and Paul. After five months' imprisonment he was a madman again, and was the second time transferred to the Kazan asylum. In May, 1887, in a period of comparative lucidity, he was joined to the batch of exiles on their march to Siberia. But before they reached Krasnoyarsk Lebedeff again became insane, and in such a state, notwithstanding the remonstrances of his companions and the certificates of the physicians, was marched to Tunka.

Another insane man in the same party was

Mavrogan, a well-known author of books on education, and formerly tutor in the Richelieu Gymnasium in Odessa. He was arrested for the first time in 1879, during General Todleben's furious reign, and without any trial, without interrogation, without explanation of the motives of his arrest, was exiled to Oriental Siberia for five years. After the expiration of this term he returned to Odessa, and a few months later he was arrested again. The charge against him was this: The spies had discovered that he had met one day in the public garden a noted revolutionist, and had a talk with him. The spies could not overhear what they were talking about, for they had to watch them at a distance; but this was deemed sufficient for arresting Mavrogan and keeping him in solitary confinement for more than a year until he lost his reason. In 1886 he was transferred to the Odessa lunatic asylum for examination. Here the well-known specialist for mental diseases, Dr. Chazky, and all his assistants, testified to his insanity. This did not prevent the police from sentencing him to four years' exile in Oriental Siberia, which order was read to Mavrogan *in the lunatic asylum* in July, 1886, by a police officer. Notwithstanding the efforts of his mother and sister, and of the medical staff of the asylum, the order was carried out. Mavrogan was transferred to the Moscow central prison, and in May, 1887, marched off to his destination.

Another similar case we will mention is that of Dobroselsky, a Pole by birth. He was arrested in Warsaw in connection with Socialist propaganda and secret printing. He lost his reason a few months after his arrest, but was, nevertheless, exiled in 1887 to Kurgan, in Western Siberia. The remarkable fact about him is that whilst sending him to his destination the authorities addressed a special request to the other exiles of Kurgan asking them to take care of their new companion *because he was insane.*

III.

ONE of the most terrible tragedies of the last two reigns—the massacre of Yakutsk—took place in connection with the practice of exiling people to the regions of Polar night. This terrible affair did not pass unnoticed and unknown, like most of the dark deeds of the Russian autocracy. Thanks to the London *Times*, it made the round of the world, marking an epoch in the story of the gradual winning over of the public opinion of England to the cause of Russian freedom.

Since that time we have received many authentic documents, explaining much that was dark and incomprehensible in the whole affair, and showing the butchery in a somewhat new light. I leave to the reader to decide whether it is a better one or worse.

At the beginning of April, 1889, thirty political exiles were waiting at Yakutsk to be transported to some locality in the extreme east of Siberia, where they were ordered to reside. These prisoners, it must be noted, were exiled by "administrative order"—that is to say, they had not been tried and convicted by any tribunal; no conclusive evidence had been adduced against them. Legally speaking, they were citizens who retained all their rights, and against whom no conviction or penalty had been inflicted. The Government—not the law, but the Government—for purely administrative reasons, had ordered these persons to live in exile. This is the way suspects against whom no evidence is forthcoming are often treated. The thirty prisoners, to reach Yakutsk, had already performed a painful and exhausting journey, lasting a whole year, and made mostly on foot by *étapes*. But to reach the further stations, such as Verkhoyansk and Kolymsk, greater hardships are in store. Some 160 miles from Yakutsk, at Aldan, the last vestiges of civilization disappear. The road crosses an absolutely desert locality, where at best a few nomad tribes may be met, though these for the most part have been decimated by smallpox.

A political prisoner who had travelled from Yakutsk to Kolymsk related that on reaching a "jurta" or resting-hut, he had only found a man dead from smallpox, another dying, and no sort of provision whatever for travellers. The other members of the family living in the hut had all fled away. Yet these huts are the only habitations to be met with on the road. They are occupied by a sort of postmaster, whose mission it is to keep open the means of communication, and who has become the only existing connexion between the Government and the natives, the latter being for the most part semi-savages. These postmasters lead a wretched life, together with their families and their cattle. The best that a "jurta" can offer to the traveller is a little shelter and a little warmth. As for food, that is altogether out of the question, and the traveller must carry his own provisions with him, or he will die of hunger. It is only on reaching Verkhoiansk that articles of primary necessity can be bought, and then at fabulous prices. But to understand better what was about to occur, it is necessary to explain further that the post-stations are at very great distances from each other. There is nothing between them but the wastes of the Polar deserts. Such distances cannot be accomplished on foot; horses drawing carriages would die of hunger, and deer alone can stand the journey. As the distance from posthouse to posthouse varies from 150 to 200 miles, there are intermediary halting-places, called "povarny," where the deer can take breath and eat their rations of moss. But for men there is no accommodation, no warmth, no shelter; no possibility of getting food anywhere. The number of deer the postmasters are by their contracts obliged to keep is calculated with a view to carrying the post once every three months, and conveying an occasional traveller. It is, therefore, quite insufficient for somewhat numerous parties; and when the deer are gone, the traveller must stop at the station or at the "povarny" and wait, sometimes for weeks, until the exhausted animals come back and are ready for use. The journey from Yakutsk to Sredne Kolymsk takes about three months, and the travellers, besides warm clothes, must have provisions for all this time, like a crew sailing for a three months' journey in the Arctic seas.

Up to the spring of 1889 the authorities at Yakutsk thought it was only right to show some leniency to the exiles under "administrative order," who were told off to the Arctic zone. They argued, and justly, that, as these latter had not been condemned to death, it was necessary to take some measures to prevent their dying of starvation on the road; therefore, to prevent the overcrowding of the post-stations, only small batches of prisoners were despatched at a time, and these at intervals of ten to fifteen days from each other. Further, to enable the prisoners to procure food for the journey, and the indispensable articles of clothing, the allowance made for the journey was paid to them ten days in advance. But as the prisoners have also to feed the Cossacks of their escort, their own allowance was not sufficient, and an advance was made to them from their monthly pay, about 10*l.* in all. These were not very great concessions, and did not prevent the occasional death from cold of several children. Cases of illness among the adults were very frequent, and some of them never recovered from the effects of the terrible journey. But all this is quite within the ordinary programme of a Russian exile's life, and they accepted all these sufferings quietly as a matter of course. Something especially ferocious and unusual must occur before protests are raised. This is precisely what happened in Yakutsk in the spring of 1889.

General Svetlizky, who, like a sensible man,

had established the above-mentioned rules for the transport of the exiles to the Polar regions, sent in his resignation of the governorship. In March of 1889 Colonel Ostashkin was appointed to fill the vacant post *ad interim*. Immediately on assuming the office of governor he thought fit to alter all the rules or customs relating to the transport of exiles under "administrative order." He decided that four instead of two prisoners should start at once, which, with the escort, made eight persons, and this at short intervals of only seven days. The money allowance for the journey was to be paid only the day before the departure, and the advance of money on the exiles' pay suppressed altogether. Further, the exiles were all to surrender themselves at the prison the day before starting, so that it would be absolutely impossible for them to make the purchases indispensable for such a journey. Finally, they were forbidden to take with them more than 200 pounds of luggage and provisions per head.

What induced Ostashkin to take such a step? In one of the letters from the exiles, these wanton cruelties are attributed to the fact that his sister was compromised in some revolutionary affair and was an exile in Siberia.

Ostashkin wanted to make amends, and show his loyalty, by a particular severity towards the political exiles. In other letters from the same source, a more lenient view is taken of Ostashkin, who is represented as a typical, narrow-minded, ignorant bureaucrat, having an implicit faith in stamped paper, and sticking to the letter of the regulations, being unable to understand or believe that they are not the perfection of human wisdom, and must be sometimes adapted to circumstances. It was prescribed, as a general rule, for exiles settled in towns, that their different allowances should be given to them at the end of the month, which could not cause serious inconvenience even to the poorest among exiles, as they could find credit for one month. The regulation prescribed, moreover, that the exiles travelling by *étapes* should not carry with them more than 200 pounds of luggage. It was not much, but there was no reason to complain, as the ordinary exiles had not to take with them any article of food, except some tea and sugar and the like. It was sheer madness to enforce such rules upon the exiles who had to embark upon a three months' journey across the icy deserts of northern Siberia. For himself and the Cossack escorting him, each exile had to take at least 480 pounds of bread alone. But men cannot stand the Arctic cold and the fatigue of such a journey on bread only. The exiles had to take with them about 200 pounds of meat, 50 pounds of butter, 20 pounds of salt—to say nothing of tobacco, tea, sugar, biscuits, etc. Besides articles of food, the exiles had 200 pounds of personal luggage: wearing apparel, linen, books, etc., which the regulations allowed them to bring with them from European Russia. How could they possibly reduce their luggage to the regulation 200 pounds? Besides, special fur coats able to stand the awful frost of 70 degrees below zero (Fahr.), are as imperatively necessary as food. In the warmest fur coat that is worn in European Russia a man would get frozen the first day of his journey.

Now Ostashkin's rules meant that the exiles should be exposed wholly unprotected both to hunger and cold.

Of course, Ostashkin did not really want to have them all frozen and starved. It was mere bureaucratic stupidity and ignorance; but this did not make the situation less dangerous. Obstinacy, official pride, which does not allow the admission of an error, and considers any expostulation as an act of insubordination, almost a personal offence—these are qualities as characteristic of our bureaucracy as ignorance and stupidity. Governor Ostashkin proved that he had the arrogance and susceptibility of all petty bureaucratic despots. To these he added cowardice all his own, which alone accounts for his mean and treacherous conduct in the later stages of this dreadful affair.

The thirty Yakutsk exiles had every reason for being alarmed at what they called the March edicts, and for taking some steps to protect themselves, their wives, sisters, and children. They received unexpected assistance on the part of the ispravnik (chief) of the district of Kolymsk, who reported to the governor that a severe epidemic of smallpox was ravaging the district through which the exiles had to travel, that many of the Yakuts holding the post stations had fallen victims to it, and that at some of them one could not put up without danger of infection.

On the 16th of March one of the exiles, Goz, went to see the governor, explaining to him that the exiles did not mean to be disrespectful or insubordinate, but that the new regulations could not be carried out without most deplorable consequences, and that they hoped that he would reconsider his decision. Ostashkin seemed impressed and even moved. "I am also a man," he said, and he promised to give his full attention to the matter. In fact, he did so. On the next day, the 17th of March, Governor Ostashkin issued several orders to the ispravnik of the district, enjoining upon him that all objects likely to cause contagion should be removed from the post stations, and that a sufficient number of relay horses and reindeers should be kept there to allow the exiles to travel without danger to their health or delay. To his bureaucratic mind to issue such an order meant to remove all difficulties. He might as well have ordered the ispravnik to have the whole road macadamised in the course of a fortnight, and bridges thrown over all the rivers, and viaducts over the ravines. These orders could have been executed by the ispravnik if he had had a magic wand to command the services of spirits. Otherwise both were equally impracticable.

The exiles knew it very well, and the orders of March 17th produced upon them the most depressing effect: nothing would be done for them, and the governor was evidently resolved to stick to his regulation. The first batch of four exiles received an order to surrender themselves to the prison authorities on the 22nd, before starting for their journey to Sredne Kolymsk, which under the circumstances was likely to be their last in this world. Exasperated at such senseless, unaccountable cruelty, the exiles assembled in the house of Notkin to discuss what was to be done in their desperate situation. Here some of the most resolute among the exiles proposed that rather than go submissively to a certain death, they would refuse to start at all, and would defend themselves arms in hand, and be killed on the spot.

We have the letter of Sophia Gurevich, written to their friends after the catastrophe, to prove that such a suggestion was made by some of the exiles. There is also an allusion to it in a letter of the widow of Hausmann. The suggestion was not accepted—a formal petition to the governor on the part of all the exiles was agreed upon. On March 21st all the thirty exiles lodged in proper quarters their petitions, couched in perfectly respectful terms.

Had the suggestions of despair been accepted and carried out the exiles would have been justified in offering resistance to a flagrant abuse of power. Only soldiers are bound to obey the orders of their superiors, even when disastrous. But if a warder or a director of a prison were to order a prisoner to do something which would infallibly lead to a fatal result, the prisoner would be justified in disobeying the order, and in resisting it, if compelled to, by force. And the exiles were not prisoners, but citizens who had not been deprived of their rights. I do not think that any English or American tribunal would hesitate in pronouncing upon their case.

But in Russia it is different; citizens have not that right of resisting the illegal actions of the administration, which is the foundation of all free constitutions. Two courses were therefore open to Governor Ostashkin, when he got wind of the suggestions made by the exiles. If he regarded them seriously, he might at once arrest the people who had supported them, and those who had heard them, and institute an inquiry. Or he might let events take their natural course, and wait until it was clear whether the exiles really meant to defend themselves or not. A handful of young men and girls could not imperil the peace of a town, with several battalions of soldiers and Cossacks. But either from cowardice or from mean calculation, Governor Ostashkin adopted a course of treachery and deceit worthy of some black chief in Africa. He deliberately laid a trap for the exiles, tranquillizing them in order to have them unprepared, and then sent armed soldiers to butcher them.

In the documents which are in our hands there is a letter from the commander of the Yakutsk Garrison, Colonel Vajev, to an intimate friend of his, in which he says that on March 21st he was summoned to the governor, who ordered him to keep his soldiers in readiness to support the police on the next day. So the use of force against the exiles was already resolved upon by Ostashkin on the 21st. Yet on this very day the chief of the Yakutsk police, Sukhachev, went to the exiles as a messenger of peace. He saw them in the morning, soon after the petitions were delivered, and then again in the evening by appointment, and he told them that *the Governor revoked, pro tem., the new regulations*, and would consider the matter carefully, and give his final resolution to-morrow morning. The chief of the police mentioned that Governor Ostashkin was very much vexed to hear that the exiles had been in a body to the offices of the police to present their petitions. This was considered too much like a political demonstration; and to prevent the recurrence of any such manifestation the exiles were told to assemble again the following day in the house of Notkin, where they would receive a definite answer. The explanation was plausible and quite in keeping with the habits of Russian officialdom. The exiles were taken in. The military ruse of Governor Ostashkin was successful; his enemies were lulled into false security, and fell into his trap with light hearts. They came to Notkin's lodgings quite unprepared either for an armed attack or for any hostility on the part of the administration.

It must be mentioned that in these regions, infested by herds of wolves, the exiles, like all other citizens, are allowed to wear fire-arms. So they might have been well-equipped for the fight, if it had been intended. But, as a matter of fact, out of the thirty-five people assembled only five happened to have their revolvers in their pockets, two of which *were not loaded.* The revolver of Notkin, the master of the house, was found in the lumber room. Two of the exiles, Bramson and Hausmann, who were declared to be the ringleaders, had left their revolvers at their lodgings. The exiles were quite unarmed, which is the best proof, if proof were needed, that the assembly was a peaceable one, and that nobody meditated offering "armed resistance." There were five visitors who, suspecting nothing, came to see their friends assembled in Notkin's house before the soldiers appeared.

And now the fatal hour arrived.

At ten o'clock in the morning, whilst the exiles were waiting for the governor's reply, a subaltern officer of the police, Olessov, came with an order to go in a body to the police, "to hear the governor's reply."

The exiles had no reason on earth to object to going once again to a place where they had been the day before. But they were naturally puzzled at the contradiction by the new order of that given to them yesterday by the chief of the police himself. They observed to Olessov that they had been especially advised by Colonel Sukhachev not to go in a body to the police office. But in reply to their observation Olessov thought it sufficient to merely repeat, "Then you are not going?" and without waiting for a reply he hastily withdrew, as one who has done all that was expected of him.

The exiles tried in vain to make him understand that they only wanted some explanation. At this juncture the troops arrived. It is an important point, upon which the account given both by the exiles and the officials are agreed, that the troops followed at the heels of the governor's messenger, and arrived a few minutes after him. This means that they were sent simultaneously with the messenger, before the reply of the exiles to his summons could be heard. It is therefore quite evident that there was premeditation on the part of Governor Ostashkin, who *wanted* to use the troops.

This conclusion is fully corroborated by the documentary evidence of the above-quoted letter of Colonel Vajev, who says that : " On March 22nd, at *ten o'clock* in the morning, I went with my soldiers to the house of Monastyrev (occupied by Notkin), *broke down* the gates and the door, and entered the room where the exiles were assembled."

Upon what followed, we have several letters from the survivors of the massacres. One of them, a man whom we know, but whose name I cannot reveal, for he is still in Siberia, writes as follows :—

" When the house was surrounded by the troops, Karamzine (the officer in command) entered the house with a platoon of soldiers, and told us that he came to escort us to the police office. We answered that the appearance of the troops appeared to us very strange, that we assembled here by the order of the governor to wait for his reply, and did not know whom to obey. The officer answered that all this did not concern him, that he was obeying orders, and that the chief of the police who was present knew everything. Here Olessov (the chief of the police) exclaimed : ' Why do you waste time in talking ? Do what you were ordered !' These words acted as a signal. The soldiers and officers became strangely excited, and Karamzine, without listening to us any longer, repeated three times : ' Will you go ?' and paying no attention to the cries : ' Yes, yes, we will go ! Give us time to dress !' (it was winter), he shouted to the soldiers : ' Take them !'

"Instantly the soldiers rushed upon us with butt ends of their guns and bayonets. Awful cries and groans filled the room. Our first row was knocked to the ground, and the next moment shots were fired on both sides. What followed immediately after I cannot say, because with the first discharge I was wounded and fell senseless to the ground. How long I lay I do not know: from what others told me afterwards, I gather that it must have been about three or four minutes. When I recovered my senses I heard no firing, and I saw that the room was empty. The platoon of soldiers had joined the troops outside, and our people rushed towards the back entrance. But it was guarded by the soldiers. The first who opened it, our dear and beloved comrade, Mukhanov, was received with a volley of balls and killed on the spot. All this happened before I recovered. When I came to my senses I felt at first no pain, but was on the contrary strangely excited, as if I were drunk. From the back room I heard the cries of distress from my companions and the groans of the wounded. I ran in that direction. But before I had gone many paces I saw the corpse of Sergius Pik, awfully mutilated, lying in a corner. He was hit by a ball in the forehead, but as if that were not enough, his lower jaw had been smashed with butt ends of guns. Horror-stricken at this sight, I rushed to another room and threw myself upon a sofa I found there. I was wounded myself. On the floor near the chimney was stretched Michael Gotz, who was severely wounded. In the corner lay Fundaminsky, wounded too, groaning pitiably and writhing with pain. The other rooms were also filled with wounded. Their groans, the sight of pools of blood everywhere, the cries of anger and terror of those who were not yet hurt, all this threw my mind into a state of prostration and misery such as no words can describe. Gradually we began to come to our senses—those who were unhurt trying to do what they could for our wounded. But all this changed in one moment. On a sudden we heard a frightful noise of a volley, and then of another, and again another. The balls were pouring upon us from all sides. The soldiers fired at the doors, windows, and walls, which were too thin to protect us against their rifles. Our people were falling one by one on all sides. The desperate cries: 'We surrender! We surrender!' resounded through the house, but the infuriated soldiers went on firing, and it was long before the commander stopped them."

There is another letter upon the same subject, whose author can be named, because he is now out of the reach of the Russian Government. It is from Zotoff, one of the three men executed on the 7th of August, 1889:—

"The beginning of the affray, as far as I can remember the details, was as follows: I clearly recollect that, before commanding 'take them!' Karamzine approached his platoon standing at the door, and said something to them in a low voice. I suppose it was some instruction, because I did not hear him say any other words but 'take them!' Yet at these words the soldiers divided in two equal parts, and made two rapid flank movements, crushing us on both sides so that we could not move. In the front row cries were heard, caused, I suppose, by the blows of the butt ends of the guns, whilst at the back some of my neighbours shouted: 'Withdraw the soldiers! we will go with the escort! give us time to put on our cloaks!' Karamzine, who was at that moment near the table, took no notice, and shouted once again to his soldiers: 'Take them!' Here something horrible occurred. The room was filled with awful heartrending cries, and several of our people fell to the ground, pierced with bayonets. I drew my revolver from my pocket, and shouted to the soldiers as loudly as I could to stop the butchery. But they did not think of heeding me. Several of them only pointed their rifles at me, and Karamzine pulled out his revolver, looking at me fixedly all the time.

"In a state of indescribable excitement I

jumped upon the sofa, and levelled my revolver at Karamzine. I do not know whether he or I fired first. I cannot tell whether anyone had fired before me. I remember only that I fired, and that there was firing on both sides; but it seems to me that all this happened simultaneously. Soon I was wounded and lost consciousness.

"When I came back to my senses, I found myself lying on the floor. I rose with difficulty, and saw that the soldiers had left the room. In a corner I perceived Pik, whose body rested against the wall, his head on his chest, a pool of blood by his side. On the floor, close by, there was a revolver. I thought he was wounded, and hastened to the next room to get some water; but, altering my mind, returned to lay him down first on the sofa. When, however, I raised his head, I perceived he was dead. He had, above the left eye, a ghastly hole from which blood and brains oozed and fell on his chest. Profoundly upset by this horrible spectacle, I hurried to the next room. There, on all sides, on the ground and on the beds, I saw the wounded, who were groaning and praying for water. Some of our friends had gathered round and tried to help them. Someone having said that there was no water in the house, but some ice in the yard, I ran out to fetch some. In crossing the third room, I saw lying on the bed Sophia Gurevitch, who had been ripped open by the bayonets. One of our comrades was placing pieces of ice on the side of the enormous wound. Her face was deadly pale, and she could hardly speak. 'Zotoff,' she murmured, 'good-bye, I am dying. I am suffering horribly. In mercy give me some poison!' I felt as if I were going mad."

The shots stopped, and the massacre seemed to be over. There was a lull for a while. Several of the exiles came out of the house asking for medical help for their wounded companions.

In the meanwhile the whole of the small town, attracted by the noise, was assembled at the gates of the besieged house. Governor Ostashkin came too. The wife of A. Hausmann tells in her letter that she came too, attracted by the sound of detonations :—

"My husband ran to me and told me that he was not hurt, but that Mukhanov was killed, and many were wounded; and he turned to the governor saying that it was disgraceful to kill people for a dispute about such a trifle as the escort. The governor replied something like 'calm yourself.' But at this moment a shot was fired at the governor by one of the exiles who had left the house."

It was Zotoff, who came to fetch a doctor, and, seeing the governor, who was the real author of all these horrors, drew out his revolver and fired two shots.

If Ostashkin had been a man with an average share of courage and self-control, he would have ordered his men to apprehend his assailant, and the matter would have stopped there. But he behaved like a coward that he was: after the first shot he turned his back and fled through the open gate. Zotoff was able to reach the house almost unhurt, although he was cribbled with balls. The soldiers were left to do whatever they chose. Not a single shot was fired from the besieged house. But for about twenty minutes the soldiers kept it under concentrated fire, the balls of their rifles piercing the door, the wooden walls, the windows—hitting the exiles in every corner. Over five hundred shots were fired by the soldiers, as was proved by the judicial inquiry. Out of the thirty-five people assembled in the house, six were killed on the spot, nine were dangerously wounded, and thirteen disabled.

Was it what Governor Ostashkin wanted? Probably it was more than he wanted. The wild beast once let loose does not stop at the mark! Anyhow, the authors of the massacre got frightened at the work of their hands. Colonel Vajev, after quoting the number of killed and wounded, exclaims, "Whose is the fault, it is not for me to say. God will judge!"

Ostashkin sent to the Governor-General of Eastern Siberia, Count Ignatiev (brother of the diplomatist), a report of the massacre, which he falsified as outrageously and as clumsily as only a man in a fit of unreasoning fear can do. For example, he conceals in his report not only the fact that about one-half of the exiles were wounded, but even that six of them were killed. That is why, in the official indictment, all the dead figure among the accused. The exiles were charged with having killed a policeman, Klebnikov, though by his own statement at his death-bed to another policeman, and by the examination of the wound, it was proved that he had been killed by mistake by the soldiers with a rifle bullet. The wounding of a number of soldiers was mentioned, though only one of them was touched with a ball, and so slightly that he did not even go to the hospital.

All this was done to make more plausible his version of the massacre of the 22nd of March, which was represented as a premeditated attack on the part of the exiles upon the soldiers sent to escort them. But Ostashkin's lies were quite gratuitous. The governor-general and the central government resolved to make a salutary example, and terrorize the whole body of Siberian exiles. And although the falsehood of Ostashkin's report was made clear in the course of a few days, the government endorsed the crime of Ostashkin, and punished the survivors of the butchery with a cruelty more shocking than that shown on the 22nd of March by the infuriated soldiers, because it was cold-blooded.

To punish the survivors for armed resistance was impossible. They had in all only four loaded revolvers. Only four persons could possibly have fired, and some of them were presumably among the six killed. The charge of premeditation and moral complicity could not be supported, because it was evident that the affray occurred unexpectedly—for the exiles at least. So that the majority of the thirty could not possibly be accused of anything worse than sending identical petitions, going in a body to the police office one day, and refusing to go thither under escort the day after—all venial offences, if offences at all, for which, according to the code of laws under which they lived, they were amenable to disciplinary punishment. This was not sufficient, and therefore the central government ordered them to be tried according to another code which makes such offences capital crimes: it is the military code for war time. When an army is face to face with the enemy a stringent discipline must be preserved. The soldiers have to obey orders, and cannot be allowed to send collective petitions or interfere in any other way with the orders of their chiefs. It is very natural that all such acts should be assimilated to open rebellion. Once we admit war we must admit its logical consequences. But what is logical for soldiers in time of war, becomes a monstrosity when applied to common citizens in time of peace, as has been done by the government with regard to the survivors of the Yakutsk massacre.

We have before us the verdict of the military tribunal instituted to judge them. Here we tread upon absolutely safe ground, for every paragraph of this ferocious document is as authentic as the three gallows and the many wrecked lives which were its consequences.

In the preamble of this verdict we are informed that, according to military code in time of war, "every open manifestation of opinion made by eight persons or more with the object of thwarting the orders of superiors, and obtaining their revocation, is *an open rebellion against the authorities.*" (Art. 263 mil. penal code, and Art. 110 in Book XX. of the military code.) In virtue of this law we read further: "The acts of the accused, who have presented in concert thirty identical petitions, asking for the repeal of the orders concerning the mode of their journey to the far north, as well as their refusal to come to the police office to hear the reply of the governor to the said petitions—*constitute acts of open rebellion intended to thwart the orders of the superiors.*"

We have translated literally, slightly condensing.

Thus the thirty exiles, by a monstrous fiction, were compared to soldiers in face of the enemy; their journey to Sredne Kolymsk, to some kind of military movement, which they refused to execute on account of its danger—a judicial joke, which would be amusing, were it not so ghastly.

The use of firearms was an aggravating circumstance, which told upon the fate of the three "ringleaders," Bernstein, Hausmann, and Zotoff.

With regard to the remaining twenty-seven, the participation in the "armed resistance" is *not even mentioned*. The five men condemned to penal servitude for life—Goz, Shender, Gurevich, Minor, and Orloff—were accused of being the most obstinate in refusing to go to the police station under escort, and the "most prominent" in presenting the collective petition. The rest, condemned to penal servitude for eight, fifteen, and twenty years, were pronounced guilty of the same offences, with extenuating circumstances, such as youth, sex, influence of others.

Two girls, Rose Frank and Anastasia Shechter, "have shown," runs their sentence, "good dispositions, and not merely consented to go under escort, but tried to persuade their companions to do the same, *and are therefore* condemned to the deprivation of all civil rights and four years of penal servitude."

It sounds like a slip of the pen, but it is only strict consistency; the two girls had atoned somewhat for their crime, still, having also sent petitions, they were "rebels," and were to be punished as such. The case of Magat makes this point still clearer; he was *not* present at Notkin's house on the 22nd March. Still, he was condemned to deprivation of all civil rights and to exile for life to the remotest parts of Siberia, because he sent a rebellious petition intending to thwart Ostashkin's orders.

Out of the thirty-five persons assembled in Notkin's house, thirty were exiles awaiting the governor's reply to their petitions, but five were mere guests, who came by chance and had nothing to do with the affair. Two of them were killed in the affray. As to the remaining three, the verdict runs thus:—"As to Kapger, Zoroastrova (a lady), and Heiman, who have sent no petitions intended to thwart the order of the governor, and arrived at Yakutsk from the country unarmed, Kapger on the eve, and the two others at 11 o'clock on the morning of March 22nd, and knowing nothing of the crimes of their companions, went to Notkin's house to see some of them, and came a few minutes before the arrival of the troops ... they are condemned: Kapger and Zoroastrova to deprivation of all privileges (as of noble birth) and civil rights, and to exile for life to the remotest parts of Siberia; Heiman (being of common extraction) to three years of imprisonment with the hardest labour that can be found for him." All this because they did not instantly obey the order of going to the police office under escort!

They had nothing to do with the affair—the order to go to the police office did not refer to them. But it was given to all the crowd, of which they happened to form a part, and they were bound to obey it instantly—always on the strength of the fiction that they were soldiers in face of the enemy and the officer Karamzine their chief. This judicial joke could certainly not be pushed farther.

The verdict of the Yakutsk military tribunal has been analyzed by us in its final form, as communicated by a telegram from St. Petersburg of July 21st, 1889, to the governor of Oriental Siberia, Count Ignatiev. It is a noteworthy fact that the central government has shown itself more cruel than the Yakutsk authorities. The Yakutsk military auditor, who had to revise the sentence of the tribunal, advised a milder punishment for many of the condemned than the one finally resolved upon by central government. Whilst in no case the prerogative of mercy has been exercised by the Tzar, the sentences of the eight women and the two boys under age have been aggravated by two or three years of penal servitude for each. Thus the central government more than approved that monstrous sentence, and, indeed, is alone responsible for it.

It is perfectly idle to inveigh against the irregularity of the judicial proceedings, the absence of counsel, and all guarantees for the accused at the Yakutsk trial. Neither counsel nor guarantee could be of any avail to the prisoners, since their acts, however innocent in themselves, came under articles which declared them capital crimes. The tribunal goes for nothing in all this story. In arbitrarily choosing the code of laws according to which the accused had to be tried, the administration chose the penalties likewise. So that we are strictly correct in saying that in the hanging of Bernstein, Hausmann, and Zotoff we have *a case of capital punishment inflicted by administrative order*, and that the rest were condemned to various terms of *hard labour also by administrative order*.

As a climax, the execution of Bernstein was

positively ghastly. Being severely wounded and unable to walk, he was taken to the gallows on his bed. The hangman fixed the rope round his neck, and then the bed was taken away and he was left to hang.

It is a relief to turn from these examples of men's cruelty, which are a dishonour to our common nature, to personal records of the three condemned men, whose last days are described to us by their comrades with religious faithfulness. They died as it is given to die only to men whose souls were filled with one great love, which purified them from all selfish and petty thoughts, and proved "stronger than death and the fear of death." There are their last letters to comrades and relatives which paint them better than any words of ours could do. By the noble courage, simplicity, and boundless devotion to their country, revealed in them, these letters can be placed by the side of Sophia Perovskaia's farewell to her mother. Yet they come from men who were rank and file people, whom we happened to hear of by mere chance—men who are true samples of the bulk of those who are persecuted in Russia, and sent to perish in the Siberian wilderness. It shows what moral strength is hidden in the hearts of young

Russia, and at what a price the present bureaucratic despotism is maintained.

Forgetful of himself, and fully absorbed by the thought of his friends, his country, and his cause, Bernstein writes:—

"My dear, my good friends and comrades,—I do not know whether I shall be allowed to wish you good-bye. I can hardly hope to do so. But in my thoughts I have said good-bye to you one and all, and I have been deeply impressed during all this time by the friendship you bore me. Let us, then, say good-bye mentally, dear comrades and friends, and let our last farewell be illuminated by the hope of a better future for our unfortunate country, which we love so well.

"Not an atom of force is lost in this world. Therefore the life of a man cannot be lost. We must never regret such a life. Let the dead bury the dead. You are united by a moral link of the highest order with your unhappy country. Do not say that your life is spent in vain because it is spent in the midst of suffering, in exile, and in prison. To suffer the suffering of one's country, to constitute a living reproach to the progenitors of evil and of darkness, surely this is a great cause, a noble work. If this should prove your last mission, you need not complain. You have brought your mite to the altar of the struggle for the freedom of our people. And, who knows, perhaps you will enjoy better days. Perhaps you will live to see the happy moment when the country, enfranchised, shall open her arms to her faithful children, who love her and whom she loves, so as to celebrate with them the feast of freedom. Then, friends, you will remember us, and this will be our great reward for all our trials. Never let this hope leave you any more than it will abandon me, even at the foot of the gallows.

"I embrace you warmly, with all my heart and all my soul.

"Yours ever,
"BERNSTEIN."

Hausmann left only a few lines:—

"I am not in a mood to write long," he says. "The thread of my thoughts is interrupted every now and then by recollections and images from the past. Let me send you from the depths of my heart a farewell and a God-speed to you and to all my companions in the struggle. If you live to rejoice at the day of common deliverance, I shall be with you in spirit, if I may use this expression. I die with unshaken faith in the triumph of justice.

"Farewell for ever, brothers,
"Yours, A. HAUSMANN."

The third of the condemned, N. Zotoff, wrote to his parents and to his comrades a few hours before the execution. His letter to his parents concludes with the following touching words:—

".... Jenny (his betrothed) has just come to pay me her visit—the last one! She has witnessed the last hours of my life, and will tell you all about it. As to myself I am unable to do it. I will only tell you that I feel very calm and even elated. But I am much tired as well, both physically and mentally: the strain upon the nerves during the last two days was so great. My dear ones, my own! Let me press you for the last time to my heart. Do not grieve about me: I die with a light heart, conscious of the justice of my cause, with a sense of strength in my breast. The only thing which saddens me is the thought of those dear ones whom I leave behind. What are my sufferings as compared with theirs? For me all will be over in a few hours. But they!— What a moral strength they must have to bear it all to the last. . . . I can hardly think of anything else when I cast a glance upon Jenny. . . . The guards have just entered. They brought me the clothes I must put on for the execution. I have already donned them, and sit in the shirt and trousers of the condemned, shivering with cold. Do not think my hand trembles from fear. But farewell, my dear ones, farewell for ever!

" Yours to the grave,
" NICHOLAS."

One would think the Yakutsk butchery must be the worst case of cruelty, brutality, and cynical lawlessness. But it is not so. Worse things have happened under Alexander III. An infamous measure was devised to terrify into submission the growing discontent. This is the so-called abolition of the distinction between political and common law prisoners. In reality it has another meaning. The position of the political prisoners has always been, and remains different from, and, except in one point, worse than that of the other offenders. They undergo the full term of their penalties in actual imprisonment, often in solitary confinement, which is never the case with felons. They are never sure of being set free after the expiration of their term, and they are more isolated and more worried with interference.

All this remains unchanged. The assimilation of political offenders to felons means, therefore, only this: that they may be flogged by order of the gaolers and administration, whereas formerly that could not be. I do not know whether the English will fully realize the terrible aggravation of the lot of our political prisoners caused by such a change. English people feel differently from Russians about corporal punishment. For us it is a mortal insult—worse than the switching across the face with a horse-whip. We speak, of course, of the educated classes. When, in 1887, General Trepoff ordered the flogging of a political prisoner, Vera Zassulitch shot him, inflicting upon him a severe wound, which was within a hairbreadth of being mortal. But the jury, which chanced to be composed of petty state officials, acquitted her, considering the flogging of an educated man an insult so unspeakable as to justify her act. Few of us are so cowardly as not to prefer twenty deaths to the degradation of such a punishment. That feeling is not a secret in high quarters. They knew perfectly at St. Petersburg what they were doing when they passed this measure. It was resolved upon in 1886, but it was finally decreed on March 8th, 1888, by an order signed by Galkin Vrassky, the head of the central prison department. This order states categorically that "no difference shall be admitted" in favour of political prisoners in respect of punishment, and that "flogging with the rod and with the whip shall be admitted."

This order was addressed to the commander of the Island of Sakhalien, and a few months later, September 23, 1888, three political exiles were flogged there.

On July 6, 1888, one of the exiles, Vasily Volnov, had been struck in the face by a certain Kamenshikov, superintendent of the central provision stores, and answered by striking his assailant in return. His twenty companions took up his case, and went in a body to their superiors to intercede in his favour. The affair was declared a rebellion, and all the twenty exiles were punished with various terms of imprisonment. As to Volnov, who was the offending party, and was under lock and key when the demonstration took place, and two other exiles, Tomashevsky and Maisner, who were the spokesmen of their companions, they were condemned by the Sakhalien administration to be flogged.

This infamous sentence was executed on the 23rd of September.

In Kara, which is the chief penal settlement in Siberia, the application of the brutal punishment has resulted in one of the most frightful tragedies on record. We have received no less than seven communications upon it from various places, one of which emanates from a friend having connections in official quarters. Besides, the fact has been officially confirmed (*Times*, March 14, 1890). So that there can be no doubt as to the main facts of this horrible story. Here are some details which are as authentic.

The tragedy of November, 1889, had its origin in events which occurred a long time ago. In August, 1888, the Governor-General, Baron Korf, while on a visit to the women's prison, entered the ward where lay Mme. Solnzeff Kovalsky, in the last stage of consumption. At the appearance of Baron Korf she did not rise from her bed, and being reminded rather roughly of her duty, she answered that it was utterly indifferent to her, whether she was in the presence of the Governor-General or a common gaoler, for she could not rise to anyone. For this want of deference the Governor ordered her to be sent to the prison of Verchny-Udinsk, and locked up in a solitary cell. A few days afterwards a police officer, Bobrovsky, who was not employed at the prison, and even did not live at Kara, but acted as a volunteer by permission of Massukov, the director of the prison, broke, with several guards, into the cell of Mme. Solnzeff Kovalsky early in the morning, while she was still in bed. Without giving her time to dress herself, they dragged her in her nightdress to the office, where she was stripped amidst the coarsest jokes, and a convict's dress put upon her.

When this fact became known to the other women, they sent a complaint, asking for the removal or punishment of the director Massukov, to the Governor-General. But as it had no effect, they resolved to have recourse to the only means of self-protection the prisoners have at their disposal—the so-called hunger strike.

The Siberian administration, though not scrupling to commit any villany which can be concealed, is much afraid of cases ending in death, which get known, stir up public opinion, and attract general attention to their actions.

Three times the women of the Kara prison resorted to this terrible weapon, but they were baffled in their efforts. The first hunger strike ended because the director Massukov informed the women that he had tendered his resignation. The fact was true, but the Governor-General refused to accept it. The women began their second hunger strike, which ended upon the false news that Massukov was removed by a telegram from the Governor to another prison. When the deception practised upon them was discovered, the women " went on strike " for the third time. It was in August, 1889. This third hunger strike lasted, according to one correspondent, seventeen days; according to another, twenty-two. It was certainly very long, for one of the women showed symptoms of raving madness in consequence of starvation. Most of the women could not move. The prison authorities threatened that they should be fed artificially if they persisted in refusing to take food.

It was at this point that Mme. Nadejda Sihida resolved to sacrifice herself in order to put an end to this intolerable condition. She had been brought to the Kara prison only a few months before, having been arrested in 1886, in connection with the printing of the *Narodnaia Volia*. Formerly she had been a superior teacher in St. Petersburg, supporting by her work her mother and a younger sister. Their family was of Greek extraction, though entirely Russianized. She was the eldest daughter, and was twenty-nine at the time of her death.

Without telling anybody of her intentions, she asked, through a guard, to see the director Massukov upon important business. On being admitted to his office she struck him in the face. Her idea was that, whatever might be her own fate, it would be impossible for Massukov, after such an insult, to keep his post. (In fact he was removed.)

Sihida was immediately transferred to the common law ward, where she was soon joined by three of her companions—Mary Kovalevsky, wife of Professor Kovalevsky, of Kiev, Miss Kolujny, and Miss Svetlizky. A report of her act was sent to the Governor-General.

She expected to be hanged; but a more terrible fate was in store for her. On the 24th of October the Kara prisoners, men and women, were assembled in their respective prisons to listen to the new decree of the Governor-General, making the political prisoners liable to corporal punishment in case of open breach of discipline.

The resolution as to Sihida's case was not yet known at that time to the prisoners, but they could already guess it.

In this extremity, hunger strikes were no longer of any avail, and the prisoners resolved to resort to another kind of strike, which we may call the strike of death!

The men, thirty in number, after hearing the new decree, declared to their director that being unable to protect themselves from such an outrage, they would destroy themselves in a body if corporal punishment should be inflicted upon any of them. They asked him to send to St. Petersburg a telegram soliciting the suspension of the new decree. But the director of the men's prison refused to risk such a step. Then the men held a consultation, at which it was proposed that, rather than live under the threat of such an ignominy, they should poison themselves in a body, in order, by such a terrible protest, to rouse public opinion, and render impossible the perpetration of the intended insult. And such was their feeling that the majority was in favour of this resolution. But a strong minority was against it, and it was resolved to wait.

They had not to wait long. On the 27th of October, three days after the promulgation of the new decree, the following order arrived from the Governor-General, Baron Korf:—" Inflict corporal punishment, according to regulation, upon Nadejda Sihida for insulting the director of the prison."

The words "according to regulation" meant that the prison surgeon had to examine the state of health of the condemned person, and testify to fitness to endure the punishment.

Being informed of the telegram, the prison surgeon, Gurvich, went to see Gomulezky, the superintendent of the common law ward, where Sihida was detained, and informed him that Sihida was in weak health, and was under his treatment for heart disease. Upon this Gomulezky telegraphed to Shamilin, the chief of the common law prisons in Oriental Siberia, that the surgeon refused to be present at the execution of the sentence. In reply to this Shamilin telegraphed: "Execute the sentence without the surgeon." But Gomulezky lingered still.

Then, on the 6th of November, there arrived

at Ust Kara, the village where the prison stands, Bobrovsky, the same officer who had distinguished himself in the affair of Mme. Solnzeff Kovalsky. He went forthwith to the prison. Half an hour later the preparations for the flogging were made.

Sihida received one hundred blows on November 6th, and on November 8th she died from the effects of the flogging.

As soon as the news of this outrage reached the men's prison, they assembled, and all the thirty (one correspondent says seventeen) took poison. Then they went to their cells. But as the quantity of poison they could smuggle into the prison was not sufficient for all, its action was slow. Two men died in the course of a few hours—Ivan Kalujny and Bobokhov. The convulsions of the dying men, and the dead silence in all the cells, aroused the guards' attention. The surgeon was summoned, and, with the help of the guards, administered emetics. No further deaths occurred.

The three women who were in the same ward with Nadejda Sihida—Mary Kovalevsky, Kolujny, and Svetlizky—poisoned themselves, and died on the day of her death.

The whole civilized world was horrified at

their ghastly story, and the Russian Government was bound to do something in order not to be considered altogether barbarous. In 1890 corporal punishment for women was abolished. But it is still maintained for men.

Thus people of refinement and education have to live under the permanent threat of this infamous outrage, which every brutal official can inflict upon them.

The question whether the torture is applied to political offenders in Russia has been often asked and discussed in the foreign press. I do not believe that mediæval torture, as such, exists in Russian prisons, and I have never supported this charge.

But is the breaking of bones and flaying alive the only form of suffering which can be called torture?

We read that the Inquisition often tortured its victims by putting them in such a position that they believed every moment to be their last. Is not the constant threat of a punishment which a certain class of people are known to consider infinitely worse than death—is not this torture in the fullest sense of the word?

IV.

NIHILISM.

I.

THE peculiar character of the Russian revolutionary movement, known under the name of "Nihilism," has been determined by the special nature of the latter-day despotism of the Romanoffs, which is unendurably oppressive for the masses, and galling in the extreme for the individual.

Neither the one nor the other of these incentives to rebellion, taken separately, could bring men to such a pitch of indignation as leads to the acts associated with the name of Nihilism. And the reader will surely admit that during the reign of Alexander III. both the stimulants were provided in very strong doses.

What have been the fortunes of Nihilism since it appeared in the fire and thunder of explosion thirteen years ago?

A STUDY OF MODERN RUSSIA. 95

But what is Nihilism ? A score of books have been written upon this subject—hundreds of magazine articles, without counting the newspapers' accounts. But up to the present the majority of the English have a very vague idea of the party which has been so much talked about. It is rather a humiliating confession for those who have been engaged for years in the production of this literature. But it is no use denying facts. The majority of generally well-informed men have very strange ideas about the so-called Nihilists. Struck by their methods and the misleading name given to them, very many people still consider them to be " Anarchists," deniers of everything, striving after destruction for destruction's sake. But, on the other hand, there are some people who have come to the conclusion that the " Nihilists " are not Socialists, but simply Radicals, striving for political freedom and constitutional forms of government. The late Charles Bradlaugh expressed such views in several of his magazine articles upon the Continental revolutionary movements, which he had studied very carefully.

Finally, there is a third set of people, and they are not few, who try to bring their sympathy with the Nihilists into accordance with their abhorrence of violent methods, by maintaining that only a small and extreme fraction of Nihilists are bomb-throwers and dynamiters, and that the "genuine article" consists of decent people, who are in favour of obtaining political freedom for their country by peaceful, even "constitutional" methods, overlooking the small detail, that the possibility of "constitutional" methods implies the existence of a constitution, which is precisely what Russia so sorely lacks.

Besides the bad name which we, Russian revolutionists, must needs use, under protest, if we want people to understand what we are speaking about—besides this name, the vagueness and contradictoriness in the general understanding of our movement is due to two causes —its complicated character on one hand, and on the other the rapid changes which it has undergone in a very short time.

Thus Mr. Bradlaugh suggests that "it is probable that in the great towns a sort of anarchist socialism is popular with the more educated speakers and writers." This is quite a mistake. Anarchism does not exist in the Russia of to-day, at all events, it is so feebly represented as to give not the slightest sign of its existence. Within the last *seventeen years* there has been not a single paper or pamphlet published in the Russian language, in Russia or abroad, in the interests of anarchism—not a single profession of faith at any of the numberless trials, not a single public manifestation of any kind. Russian socialism of the last decade is entirely social democratic. But only fifteen or seventeen years ago the whole of socialist Russia was anarchical; although this anarchism, as the reader will presently see, had nothing whatever to do with the dynamite Anarchists of modern times.

This is not the only transformation which has taken place in our movement. It was propagandist in 1873-7, terrorist in 1878-9; in 1880-2 it was chiefly military, and not unlike the Spanish patriotic movement; and it has become to a large extent civil and popular once again within the last eight years. It is on the eve of a new transformation nowadays, and there is no saying whether it will become military, civil, or terroristic, or all the three combined.

The primitive and genuine Nihilists, those who actually bore that name in Russia, and to some extent deserved it, were a philosophical and ethical school, long ago extinct in Russia, which has been immortalized by Turgueneff in his novel, " Fathers and Children."

The intellectual movement, of which Bazaroff is a living impersonation, sprang up in our country in the epoch following the Crimean defeat, which marks a general breaking down of the despotic *régime* of Nicholas.

Serfdom, recognized as the source of Russia's poverty, weakness, and of the low standard of public morality, was abolished in 1861—and the country turned over a new leaf. The enfranchisement of the millions of peasantry was a measure that revolutionized the entire moral, economic, and social life of our country. Not peasants alone were slaves in Russia in the old times. The absolute uncontrolled power of the serf-owners, who formed the bulk of the cultured and governing class, produced certain habits of despotism which extended to all the spheres of national life. The children were slaves to their parents, the wives to their husbands, the petty officials to their superiors, the employed to the employer. A good education was no guarantee against the vitiating influences of this immoral institution. It was at this time that the French, who had to deal with the most cultured part of Russian society, said that one only needs to scratch a Russian to find a Tartar. Tartars our fathers were, the varnish of civilization notwithstanding, and their families knew it better than anyone else.

The abolition of serfdom, the worst form of dependency of men upon men, was the signal for a general rising of all the oppressed part of the community. There was throughout all Russia a universal outburst of rebellion against all sorts of dependency, all authority imposed upon men's freedom in the domain of personal conduct as well as in the domain of thought. The individual, tired of oppression, rose in all his pride and power, breaking the chains of ancient traditions, and recognizing no other guidance but his individual mind.

Such were the true Nihilists, the destroyers, who did not trouble themselves about what was to be built after them.

They did not exactly deny everything, for they believed firmly, fanatically, in science and in the power of the individual mind. But they thought nothing else worth the slightest respect, and they attacked and ran down family, religion, art, and social institutions, with all the more vehemence the higher they were held in the opinion of their fellow-countrymen.

Something similar took place in Germany in the so-called "Sturm und Drang" period, and for similar reasons. But the Germans of the first quarter of this century had not so much to destroy, and they had not the same lust for destruction: there was much in their past they had reasons to love and respect. Besides, in those days, European science and philosophy had not at their command such lethal weapons of destruction as were put at the service of the Russian Nihilists in the second half of this century.

Thus, Nihilism proper, the Nihilism embodied in Bazaroff, was a genuine Russian apparition. It was an impassioned protest against the former annihilation of the individual. With all its exaggerations and mistakes it was a grand movement, for its basis was sound, and its effect most beneficial in a country like ours.

Nihilism of Bazaroff's type was dead and buried about ten years before the starting of the present revolutionary movement. No one denies art and poetry nowadays, no one wears ugly dresses on principle, no one protests against the idea of men's duties towards the community. No one preaches against the obligations imposed upon people by family life. But there is no country where the relations between parents and children and men and women are based to such an extent upon the principle of equality, and there is no society so broad-minded and tolerant as the Russian. Much of this is due to the gallant struggle of the early Nihilists, who were the first to engraft upon Russia the proud Western conception of individuality which struck root, and will spread with every generation.

It is impossible not to see a close relationship between the early Nihilism and the present militant one, in which the old spirit of personal independence is revived, coupled this time with social feeling, urging the individual to sacrifice himself for the many who feel and suffer like himself. But in its state of absolute purity, unalloyed with any social feeling, stern and fierce as expounded by Bazaroff, Nihilism could not stand for long. The Russians are the least individualistic of all people in Europe, the feeling of organic union with their countrymen being with them the strongest feeling. The striving for individual happiness, however refined, could not suit their sympathetic gregarious nature, craving for works of devotion to others. Even in the palmy days of Nihilism of Bazaroff's school, there was in the movement an undercurrent making for another direction. It may be called social Nihilism, as opposed to the individualistic, and was represented in 1860 by Nicolas Tchernyshevsky, the publicist, journalist, economist, and novelist, whose name is familiar to all those who have studied the Russian question.

Tchernyshevsky was a socialist, and the father of the Russian revolutionary movement. He preached the absolute devotion of the individual to the cause of regeneration of his country. Only he gave the idea of self-sacrifice an individualistic interpretation. "All men's actions," he said, "are stimulated by egotism, and have no other scope except individual happiness. But one person whose intellectual and moral standard is low finds his pleasure and happiness in making money or in drinking or over-eating himself, whilst another is happy in doing good to his fellow men, in dying, if necessary, for their sake." And Tchernyshevsky went on scoffing at and ridiculing self-sacrifice as a logical absurdity, while preaching it passionately in practice. The theory of moralized egotism and egotistical self-abnegation was developed by Tchernyshevsky and his followers with admirable skill and dialectical subtlety, and served as a transition to the doctrine of absolute devotion to the good of the community, which the next generation transformed into a sort of religion.

As time went on the influence of Tchernyshevsky gained ground upon that of the genuine Nihilism, represented by Pisareff, a young highly gifted journalist, and the writers grouped around him. The generation of 1870 was entirely educated by Tchernyshevsky, but it took from him only the kernel of his ethics, dropping as useless and cumbersome his theory of all-pervading individualism.

A new conception made its way at this epoch into social science, in opposition to the former individualistic theory of social contract for securing mutual individual happiness: that of the integrality of the body politic, in which individuals are but transitory parts. Its source is to be traced to Auguste Comte, the father of Positivism, whose philosophical theories (not religion) found a ready acceptance in Russia. But its chief propagator in Russia was undoubtedly Herbert Spencer, whose works have all been translated into Russian, and exercised a great influence upon the mind of our generation.

The idea of duty towards the community

threw into the background that of the duty of the individual towards himself.

A little volume, which appeared at this epoch, embodied this new tendency very forcibly and consistently. It was from the pen of Peter Lavroff, the present refugee in Paris, then professor of mathematics in one of the St. Petersburg military academies, and bears the modest title of "Historical Letters." Its leading idea is that of the enormous indebtedness of the cultured minority to the masses, who in the course of centuries have toiled and suffered, undergoing indescribable privations in order that a small minority might be able to cultivate their minds, and transmit to their children the accumulated inheritance of knowledge and moral and intellectual refinement.

To work for the good of the people ceases to be a pleasure in which a man can indulge or not, as he chooses. It becomes a stringent duty he is bound to fulfil, and for which he cannot claim much credit to himself. It is the simple repayment of the debt he has contracted in accepting the inheritance so heavily paid for by the mass of the people.

Another writer, Schapov, whose name is little known abroad, must be mentioned here, because his influence in shaping the views of our generation can be compared only to that of Tchernyshevsky. Schapov is the historian of the Russian peasantry. He was professor of history in the Kazan University up to 1862, when he was arrested, and exiled to Siberia, for a speech made at a great street demonstration organized to protest against the slaughter of peasants in the Bezdna district.

This great demonstration brought Schapov's name for the first time into public notice. His works appeared afterwards, forming a brilliant sequel to such a beginning.

Schapov's philosophy can be best described as the modern incarnation of *Slavophilism*, purged of monarchial superstition and orthodox bigotry. He is national without being a partisan either of Tzardom or of the orthodox church. All his erudite works are devoted to the study of the past history of the Russian people. His object is to bring to light the constructive principles of political and social life, adhered to by the masses of the peasantry as opposed to those which the Muscovite, and afterwards the St. Petersburg monarchy forced upon them. These principles are self-government and local autonomy in political and ecclesiastical matters, as opposed to the administrative and ecclesiastic centralization of the State. In the economical domain, it was communistic ownership of land, meadows, forests, fisheries, and all natural riches, as opposed to the private property inculcated by the State. In the chaotic popular movements of the past he has discovered system and harmony, showing the masses of the Russian peasantry to be an excellent plastic material for the building up of a State, very different from the one which temporary historical necessity has actually constituted.

But this historical necessity has become a thing of the past, whilst the peasants have remained unchanged. The conclusion from this might be easily drawn.

Schapov's voluminous and rather heavy works (written in an atrocious style) have been studied with avidity by the entire advanced youth of our generation. Except Tchernyshevsky, no writer has had such a deep and lasting influence upon our intellectual movement. He gave a solid, scientific basis to the whole literature upon the modern peasants, so extensive and varied, numbering among its writers the most gifted men of our literary generation. They all belong to Schapov's school, confirming with regard to modern peasantry what Schapov discovered with regard to their ancestors.

Educated Russia has always been democratic, we may say, *peasantist*, in her feelings, and not without cause. The peasant class is not merely the most numerous, but the soundest, bravest, and most thoroughly original of our classes. To prove that this is not a dream of democratic enthusiasts, we have only to refer to our famous novelists, who in their quality of great artists are above suspicion of exaggeration or misrepresentation. Their collective work is a revelation of Russia, as a whole, in which the peasants have a conspicuous place of their own. Now Turgueneff's sketches, collected in the "Sportsman's Sketches," Dostoevsky's "Buried Alive," and Tolstoi's numerous scenes and stories from peasant life, show us a series of living types which command respect, sometimes admiration, and testify to the great gifts and the vast amount of moral energy hidden in the masses of our common people.

The writers of the past generation have prepared the ground for the young ones, creating that powerful, peculiarly Russian, democratic feeling, which is the mainspring of our revolutionary movement. The idea of duty towards the people, and of the historical debt of the educated minority towards the masses, was readily accepted by our sensitive, impressionable youth, as a new basis for their ethics. Still, it was an abstraction, a dry reasoned-out conception, which could not stir men's hearts. But thanks to the above-mentioned writers, the idea of the people assumed a concrete palpable form, appealing alike to reason, enthusiasm, and pity.

With our emotional, sympathetic people, it became a momentous impulsive power, urging them to gladly give up wealth, personal preferment, even life, provided they could give some relief to the people whom they thought so great, and knew to be so unfortunate.

And now the socialists of the West came to tell the young enthusiast that there is a way to solve the social question and remove for ever the causes of popular sufferings. These theories appeared as the last word of social philosophy, sanctioned by the authority of the greatest names in economical science, and by the adhesion of many hundred thousand workmen of the international socialism, standing at the head of the world's democracy.

The Russians jumped at it as at a new revelation. The new apostles found their gospel, for which henceforward they would live and die.

II.

From 1870, the Russian Revolution ceases to be something apart, and becomes a branch of international socialism, which, at that epoch, descended from the clouds, and became for the first time the embodiment of the working men's aspirations. Still, the peculiar conditions of our country gave to the Russian socialist movement a somewhat different shape and history.

At that time, as nowadays, international socialism was divided into two sections, the social democrats and the anarchists. The former advocated the abolition of private property in the instruments of labour and their collective ownership by the workmen. But they wanted to preserve the present political organizations, which should be made an instrument for the economical rebuilding of the State. Thus, for the social democrats the practical object was to take possession of political power.

Peaceful electoral agitation was their chief weapon, the element of physical revolution being admitted only incidentally, if at all.

The anarchists, headed then by our countryman, Michael Bakunin, were in favour of a total remoulding both of economical and of political organization, advocating the total abolition of the State, and the substitution for it of a series of small, absolutely independent and freely constituted communes. Parliamentary institutions were for them of no possible use, and they relied for the realization of their ideals entirely upon the spontaneous action of the masses risen in rebellion.

Of these two doctrines, the last had by far the greater fascination for the Russian socialists of 1870. It promised more, for to abolish at one stroke men's economical and political bondage, was like killing two birds with one stone. Then it made of no account the political backwardness of Russia, which appeared rather more favoured than other countries. The antiquated autocracy was easier to overthrow than a constitutional monarchy based upon the popular vote. According to Bakunin the village "Mir" had only to be freed from the oppressive tutorship of the State to become an ideal form of anarchical government by all with the consent of all.

The Russians are very subject to spiritual contagion, and often accept or drop a theory in a body. In 1870 the whole of advanced Russia was anarchist. The autocracy was opposed simply because it was a government, no substantial difference being admitted to exist between Russian autocracy and, let us say, the English parliamentary *régime*. Accordingly, nothing was expected, and nothing was asked, from the educated classes and the liberal opposition, which was in favour of a constitutional government for Russia. The socialists of this epoch based all their hopes upon the peasants. Thousands of young people of both sexes went upon a crusade amongst the peasants; the more exalted with the object of calling them to open rebellion, the more moderate with the intention of preparing the ground for the future revolution by peaceful socialist propaganda. This was one of the most touching and characteristic episodes of the young movement, when the motto "all for the people and nothing for ourselves" was the order of the day.

Most of the young enthusiasts—for they were all young—belonged to the upper classes. The peasants, for whose awakening they proposed to give their all, had been the serfs of their fathers. The feeling of suspicion towards their former masters was so strong as to render utterly hopeless any attempt on the part of the "gentlemen" to obtain any influence among the common people. The propagandists therefore renounced all their privileges, and became themselves common manual labourers, workmen and workwomen in the fields, at the factories, at the wharves and railways, in all places where common workpeople assembled. They supported cheerfully all hardships and privations, and considered themselves amply repaid for all their trouble if they succeeded in winning here and there some adherents to their cause.

This socialist crusade was a complete failure. The peasants only opened their eyes with wonder at the summons to rebellion, on the part of strangers, who came nobody knew from whence, and wished nobody knew what. They lent, it is true, a very willing ear to the propaganda of socialism. But there was no way of getting adherents without attracting the attention of the police, in a country where everything is watched. In the course of 1873-4, fifteen hundred propagandists and agitators, or their friends and supposed accomplices were arrested in the thirty-seven provinces of the Empire, and thrown into prison. One-half of them were released after a few months' detention; the rest were kept in preliminary confinement for from two to four years, during which seventy-three of them either died or lost their reason. In 1877 a part of them (193) were tried and condemned to various punishments, from simple exile to ten years of hard labour in the Siberian mines.

This was a death blow to anarchism. Whatever may be one's views upon the best form of society in the future, it was evident that in the present the political question was not so irrelevant to the cause of the workers themselves as the early socialists tried to believe. Thousands of lives were wrecked for saying in private things which are proclaimed from the house-tops in all free countries. The propagandists who were ready to devote their lifetime to the work of enlightening the people, were not allowed to devote to it more than a few days, sometimes a few hours. Political freedom was evidently something worth having, be it only for the sake of enabling the people's friends to be of some use to them.

But theories, once adopted, do not disappear so easily. The passions spoke first; and men began to act in the right direction before they had reasoned out their action. The wanton cruelty with which political prisoners were treated, the horrors of preliminary detention, the barbarous punishment inflicted for offences so trifling, all this proved unendurable even to the mild, patient Russians. The spirit of revenge was kindled, giving birth to the first attacks upon the government, known by the name of terrorism. It began by an act of individual retaliation which, under the circumstances, had all the dignity of a solemn act of public justice. A girl, Vera Zassulitch, shot General Trepoff, who ordered the flogging of a political prisoner. On March 31, 1878, she was acquitted by the jury, though she never denied her act. In 1878, terrorism was accepted as a system of warfare by the most influential and energetic section of Russian revolutionists grouped around the paper *Zemlia and Volia* (Land and Liberty). But at first this practical struggle with political despotism was carried on under the banner of anarchy. "The question of constitution does not interest us," said the terrorists of this epoch in their pamphlet and in their paper, *Land and Liberty*, "the essential part of our activity is the propaganda amongst the people. In striking the worst amongst the officials we merely want to protect our companions from the worst treatment by the government and its agents. The terrorists must be looked upon as a small detachment protecting the bulk of an army at some dangerous passage."

This attempt to find a way out of the contradiction between theory and practice could not hold its position for long, because it was illogical on the face of it. Since it was recognized that the socialist propaganda, to be effective, needed protection against wilful interruption, the natural course to follow was to obtain such changes in the political constitution as would give it the permanent and real protection of the laws. As to terrorism, whatever its ultimate effect upon the government, its immediate consequences could not be other than the aggravation of severities and the increase of the obstacles to peaceful socialist propaganda. In fact, the attempt to reconcile the irreconcilable was soon abandoned, and a few months later, in 1879, there came a split in the revolutionary party. A small fraction stuck to the old banner, and declared against both political action and terrorism, and for the continuation of simple propaganda, notwithstanding the overwhelming odds against it. It grouped itself around a paper called *Tcherny Perediel*. This party had but a small following, and did nothing of importance. The paper also had but a short life, being detected in January, 1880, a fortnight after the publication of its only number. In 1888 it was resuscitated abroad, where it is published up to the present time in the form of a magazine, now bearing the title of *Social Democrat*, with the most orthodox social democratic programme. Of this new departure we will speak later on.

Now we will follow the fortunes of the majority which made a step forward, having written plainly upon their banner the political emancipation of their country as the immediate object of the revolutionary party. They founded the paper *Narodnaia Volia*, and constituted the party of the same name, which may be considered the embodiment of "Nihilism," as understood abroad. It was that body, with the famous Executive Committee at its head, which was at the bottom of all the Nihilists' attempts and conspiracies.

In proclaiming political revolution its immediate aim, the Narodnaia Volia party did not renounce socialism. But it certainly had to renounce the last traces of anarchism it may have retained. When once the necessity of fighting for political freedom was recognized, it was natural to consider how to take the best possible advantage of representative institutions in the future. This means to utilize them as an instrument of reforms, as well as a protection of the propaganda preliminary to those reforms. Thus the Russian anarchists, by the very logic of their position, were converted into social democrats. The programme of the Narodnaia Volia issued in 1880, the year after the split, shows the rapidity and thoroughness of this change. It is above all a programme of political reform, its requisites being :—

1. A permanent representative assembly, having the supreme control and direction in all general State affairs.

2. Provincial self-government secured by the election of all public functionaries.

3. Independence of the village commune ("Mir") as an economical and administrative unit.

4. Complete liberty of conscience, speech,

press, meetings, association, and electoral agitation.

5. Manhood suffrage.

6. Substitution of a territorial militia for the standing army.

This was their political programme. The economical programme is summed up in two paragraphs :—

7. Nationalization of land.

8. Series of measures tending to transfer the possession of factories to workmen.

These paragraphs make the programme a socialistic one, but it is strictly social democratic. The element of physical force plays a part only in the political revolution. The re-moulding of the country's economical organization is understood to be carried on exclusively by legislation.

This programme differs from that of the social democrats of other countries in the greater stress laid upon agrarian reform. Its authors do not think Russia sufficiently developed industrially to advocate the immediate introduction of collective ownership by the workmen of factories and industrial concerns— and we think they are right in this. They undoubtedly are right on the other hand in considering the Russian peasantry fully competent to carry out any land nationalization scheme. Thus it may be said that so far as economics is concerned Nihilism is social democracy proposing to begin its work from the other end. This party is called in Russia National Socialists (*Sozialisty Narodniki*) by way of distinction from the social democrats proper, who have recently appeared in Russia.

The true distinction of the Russian Nihilists as a body lies, however, not in their methods of carrying out social reforms, but in the fact that for the time being they had to put off the idea of social reforms and devote their energies to a political struggle. The Russian Nihilists may be described as a branch of International Social Democracy, which took the lead in the struggle for political freedom in Russia.

The peasants, owing to their ignorance and the vastness of the areas over which they live scattered, cannot be effectively appealed to in the present phase of our revolutionary struggle. The Russian revolution is a town revolution, and has to find its support in the townspeople, who understand and desire political freedom. These are the educated Russians of all classes, including the workmen of big towns as well as representatives of the privileged classes. The Nihilist efforts to achieve that great national end have been of a double nature—partly destructive, partly constructive. The first need not be dwelt upon long, for it had an echo all over the world. It consisted in a series of attempts against the Tzar, which profoundly stirred the whole of educated Russia, brought forward the political question to the exclusion of everything else, and divided Russia into two hostile camps, between whom at one moment victory seemed vacillating.

The constructive work of the Nihilists is represented by their efforts to take advantage of a time of public excitement to organize a body of conspirators strong enough to attempt an open military revolution. This part of the Nihilists' activity is less known and little appreciated, because they did not succeed in carrying it to a practical result; yet it is certainly very remarkable what difficulties were overcome. The years 1881–82 mark the nearest approach of the Russian revolution to an actual insurrection similar to that of the Decembrists in 1825. From 1880 the revolutionary ideas began to make rapid progress in the army, especially in the St. Petersburg garrison and Kronstadt navy. An important secret organization was founded, headed by some patriotic officers, such as Lieutenant Sukhanov and Baron Stromberg in Kronstadt, and Captain Pokhitonov and Rogatchev in St. Petersburg. Scores of officers of all arms and different grades joined the conspiracy, which very soon extended its ramifications all over the empire. It included men of the highest reputation and brilliant military antecedents, such as Colonel Michael Ashenbrenner, the above-mentioned Captains Pokhitonov, Stromberg, and many others, some of them commanders of independent corps. The soldiers were at the same time approached by socialist workmen, who made propaganda in their midst. In one important body of troops I will not particularize, but one which was in possession of guns, it occurred that the two rival revolutionary organizations, the *Narodnaia Volia* and the *Tcherny Perediel*, happened to have worked simultaneously without knowing it, the first among the officers, the latter among the privates. Both were so successful that after a time the two streams met. One morning one of the officers coming unexpectedly to the barracks, noticed that the soldiers were reading some newspaper, which they hastily concealed under the table at his appearance. He was curious to know what it was, and ordered the paper to be handed over to him. It was a fresh number of the *Tcherny Perediel*. He said nothing, and took the copy with him to show his companions his discovery. The soldiers considered themselves irretrievably lost. Great was their delight when a few days later they learned from their friends in the *Tcherny Perediel*, with whom the *Narodnaia Volia* communicated, that they had nothing to fear, because their officers were their brethren in the cause. The result was a deputation on the part of the privates, which respectfully informed their commanders that they were quite willing at any given moment to appear before the Palace with their guns and make it a heap of ruins in a quarter of an hour.

In several other independent bodies of troops the revolution was so strongly represented as to render almost certain the adhesion of the whole body at the decisive moment. The military organization had its own central committee, independent in all its interior affairs, but all the military conspirators were pledged by a solemn oath to rise in arms at the bidding of the Executive Committee, and come to the place assigned to them with as many of their men as they should be able to bring with them.

One word would have sufficed to effect an actual military rising. But this word was not uttered, and no action took place.

The spread of revolutionary feeling was so rapid in the army that the Central Committee hoped to be able to strike a great blow and make the insurrection a successful one. The rising was deferred from week to week, and from month to month, until the Government got wind of what was brooding, and arrested the leaders of the military conspiracy in St. Petersburg, and then laid hands on many of their affiliated circles in the province, thus rendering any action impossible.

No one is to blame for these fatal procrastinations. It is such a tremendous responsibility to decide upon a premature insurrection, likely to serve as a good example, but doomed beforehand to failure and blood suppression, when a short delay gives fair promise of a success. Conspiracies are like games of chance, in which the keenest foresight is of no avail against the caprice of fortune.

The years 1882-3 present a series of attempts

at readjusting the broken threads of conspiracies. But disasters, once begun, followed in rapid succession. About 250-300 officers of all arms were arrested all over the empire, one-third of them belonging to the garrison of St. Petersburg and Kronstadt. Most were young officers of the first three grades. But there were in their midst two colonels, two majors, and a score of captains and lieutenant-captains.

The military organization was broken, and the committee was not able to muster sufficient forces, even for a serious demonstration.

The year 1884, and the following ones, are those in which militant Nihilism passes through the most critical period of its existence. Conspiracies go on uninterruptedly, but they are so weak that they rarely ripen into actual attempts. Only on one occasion, namely, in March, 1887, the conspirators were able to come down into the streets with their bombs. The revolution has practically entered into a new phase.

III.

Is Russia ripe for political freedom ? Do the Russian people want a representative Government, and are they enlightened enough to use parliamentary institutions properly if they get them? These are the fundamental questions which every thinking man, whether Russian or foreign, must decide for himself before he takes up any position or line of conduct in Russian politics.

It is evident that if Russia is not ripe for political freedom, it is sheer madness to attack autocracy, and idle sentimentalism to inveigh against the evils of a political system which is the only one possible for the country.

I expect the reader will not be surprised if I say that for thinking men in Russia the point is no longer open to question. But that it is so with foreigners, we have quite recently had innumerable proofs.

Alexander III.'s death made Russian internal affairs the topic of the day, and gave us the rare opportunity of hearing the opinions of hundreds of eminent men in this country. Now these intellectual statistics, thus gathered, have given us abundant proofs that with the majority of English people the obstacle to their frank sympathy with the cause of Russian freedom lies precisely in the idea that Russia is not yet fit for a constitutional government.

One cannot expect foreigners to know much

about the real conditions of a country like Russia, which makes no claim as yet to have taken an active part in the great work of common culture. And, in fact, we do not find evidences of any great study of Russian affairs in the numerous speeches, sermons, and newspaper articles which recommend patience and self-restraint to us on the ground that the time has not yet come for us to claim our share of freedom.

The reasoning we find at the basis of this easy resignation is invariably this:—Autocracy exists in Russia, consequently it must suit her people, otherwise they would have changed it.

Yes, undoubtedly; in the long run, a country gets the government wanted by her people. But we must not forget that the process of readjustment is not everywhere equally easy and speedy. Where there are representative institutions, this readjustment is as effective as it is prompt, operating regularly and peacefully through the ballot-box. But the readjustment is slow and painful in countries where people have to send their votes by volleys of insurgents, by attacks of crowds of rebels, or by the bombs of conspirators.

It takes long to obtain such a vote, and to get

it properly registered, and, what is worse, as time advances, the difficulties of the method increase, as well as the terrible expenditure of blood and human suffering necessary for this sort of electoral agitation.

It was comparatively easy for the English to wrest their freedom from their weak kings. The French had a harder struggle, but they were able to overcome them completely at one stroke, the forces of Louis XVI. being inferior to those of one single regiment of to-day, armed with modern weapons.

Neither the Austrians nor the Germans succeeded in 1848 in getting anything like the French share of freedom, their struggle for political rights going on until now.

Needless to say how much more arduous is, in this respect, the position of Russia, which is the last comer in the struggle for the right of man.

Russian autocracy can make a much stronger resistance than any previous tyranny. This means that the Russian people must outgrow her Government much more completely than either Germany or France, before they can force it into harmony with their new wants and new aspirations.

The fact that autocracy exists is an obvious and unmistakable proof that the forces of the opposition are not yet strong enough to overcome it. If that is what is meant by those who speak of Russia not being "ripe" for freedom, they are certainly quite right. But we do not get much light upon the present condition of Russia or her future prospects by the restatement of such obvious and self-evident truths.

It seems to me that what the English ought to know is what stage autocracy is in, how far the organic growth of the country has prepared her for national self-government, independently of the unforeseeable chances of success.

Nobody will maintain that autocracy is in its heyday in Russia: the signs of bitter, fierce dissatisfaction are too many for that. But still there are people who suppose that it has taken deep root in the country, because the masses of the peasantry are supposed to be deeply monarchical and too ignorant to be able to appreciate and use free institutions.

There is a great eagerness for education among the Russian peasantry, which the Russian Government does its best to check. But there is as yet little book-lore among them.

Only one man out of ten can read, and only one boy out of fourteen can get admission to any school. But the unimpeachable evidence of statistics shows that in Austria, in 1863, fifteen years after the advent of constitutional *régime*, the percentage of illiterate people was exactly the same as in Russia of to-day.

The French peasants in 1789 were undoubtedly worse educated than those of modern Russia. So were the Italians in 1860. And it may be doubted whether the mass of the English were ahead of us in this respect in the time of the Commonwealth. One must not exaggerate the importance of book-lore. Deficiency in that does not mean stupidity or barbarism. Certain precepts and rules of life, evolved in a nation in the course of generations and transmitted from father to children, are much more important for the building up of a state than the power of reading a newspaper or cheap book or of writing a letter. Now, in this respect, the Russian peasants have been more favoured than the rural classes in many more advanced nations. They have had from time immemorial some experience of self-government, on a small scale, in their village communes, where all common affairs are managed by assemblies of all the householders.

In 1864, three years after the emancipation, being called to take part in self-government of a higher order, the peasants gave proofs of their qualifications as citizens, which were as striking as the moderation and democratic tolerance exhibited on the same occasion by our upper classes.

Imagine the Virginian and Georgian slaves summoned to sit in some council side by side with their former masters, discussing and voting as their equals. What conflicts would it not lead to? In Russia they worked in perfect harmony, no disorder being ever recorded, the peasant deputies, after a very short time, fully entering into the spirit of their new functions.

Provinces like Viatka and Perm, where there was hardly any landed nobility, and where, consequently, the peasant delegates formed the majority, were among those where the zemstvos worked best.

These are conclusive facts. It would be absurd to pretend that our peasants have reached the high level of the Swiss, Norwegian, or American agricultural classes, or of the mass of English workmen. But it would be no exaggeration to say that, such as they are now, they are better prepared for a proper use of political freedom than the masses were in any of the great European countries at the time when their free institutions were started.

And what of their much talked of loyalty? What of their devotion to the Tzar?

The peasants have never been asked to express themselves on this delicate point. Count Tolstoi assures us that it is all twaddle. The peasants, he says, care for their cabbages more than for their Tzar, and would prefer good land with the Sultan to rule over them, to bad land with the White Tzar.

Anyhow, it is quite certain that the land and cabbages are at the bottom of this loyalty to the Tzar. Regardless of all proofs to the contrary, the peasant is firmly persuaded that the Tzar means to give him, some day, plenty of land and cabbages, and the best of everything, and that his land is held back from him only by the wicked officials.

Now this sort of monarchism is the political creed of the masses in all lands, not only before but long after the establishment of free governments.

The masses drop this creed when they cease to be the masses, by which I mean when there is no longer any distinction between the townspeople and country people.

People who are like children in their simplicity of mind and the vividness and freshness of their imaginations, must be children in their political conceptions as well. Peasants cannot understand, and nowhere do they understand, the complicated machinery of parliamentary governments, with its balance of power and their mutual checks. But the figure of a king, tzar, or emperor appeals to their fancy, to their minds, and to their hearts as well. The picturesque idea of personal power it conveys is invariably associated with that of benevolence. They cannot realize that a man having all power should not wish to do his people every good. These are the elements out of which the universal monarchical legend is built up. It lingers in the rural districts of the constitutional monarchies of the Continent, such as Italy and Austria. The people there have been sending, for a generation or two, their deputies to parliament, yet still consider the King or Kaiser as their true friend, and look upon their representatives as a body of gentlemen of whom nobody knows exactly what they have in mind.

This legendary monarchism has not, in these cases, interfered with the working of parliamentary institutions, nor has it prevented the success of revolutions. The masses of the French people were deeply monarchical at the end of the last century, whilst monarchy was being demolished in their capital. Hardly different was the condition of England in the time of the Commonwealth.

Free political institutions have been through all the world the result of the work of the educated minorities. The people know very well the difference between a good and a bad government, because they feel it on their skins. But it has been for the educated minorities to devise and carry out a more satisfactory political system, as it is for the physician to offer a remedy for his patient's disease.

Thus the question whether Russia is ripe for political freedom is reduced to this: Whether her educated class, as a body, understands and cares for freedom, and whether they are able and willing to carry on a free government for the general good of the nation.

To put this question is to solve it. The

educated class in Russia is counted nowadays by millions, and, as far as knowledge and talent go, can hold its own by the side of the corresponding class of any other nation. In fact, this class makes Russia a European country. Our science, literature, periodical press, and our schools are European.

In the number of books published yearly, Russia stands third in the list of great European nations, being inferior, in this respect, only to France (11,000) and Germany (10,000), whilst surpassing Austria and Great Britain.

There are more solid works in Russia than in most other countries. Fiction and theology make a comparatively small item in our publishers' lists. As to Russian monthlies, numbering their readers by scores of thousands, they are true cyclopædias of varied knowledge. The proportion of people of a university education in our professional and literary class is greater than in any continental country except Germany.

There is an over-production of higher educated people, to use the expression of the reactionary press, which clamours for further restrictions of the right of admission to the universities, on the ground that men of high culture, unable to find employment, naturally become disaffected.

Indeed, with the present misery of the people, hundreds of scientific agriculturists and technologists cannot find a use for their capacities, whilst agriculture is at the same stage as it was in the sixteenth century, and out of a hundred people who die, only four have medical attendance of any kind. But this fact speaks against the system, and not against the Russian educated class.

Bureaucratic despotism has created an elaborate system of checks and barriers with the object of hindering the access of the educated class to the people as completely as possible, and even of excluding from them altogether that section which is likely to be most devoted to the people, and presumably more useful on account of its enthusiasm for democratic ideas. The privilege of serving the people is restricted to those whom property qualifications or ignorance have made selfish and narrow-minded. Only the richer section of the nobility are allowed to take part in the Zemstvos, or provincial councils; the poorer and more democratic, which is as a rule the better educated section of the nobility, is excluded. In municipal self-government a professor of a university has no voice in the elections, no matter how long he may been a resident in the town, whilst every ignorant shop assistant is supposed to become a fully qualified voter the day after he takes his stand behind the counter. A well-educated man can never get a post as village schoolmaster or commercial clerk, but it will be readily given to a retired soldier who can hardly spell.

Thus, leaving alone the question of the terrible havoc caused by the political persecutions among the best and ablest and most devoted friends of the people, we find that the laws are so framed as to utilize but a small part of the intellectual power and civic devotion of our educated class.

Yet if we take the work which this class has been allowed to do in such unfavourable conditions in the Zemstvos, municipalities, statistical boards, relief committees, and societies of every description, and compare it with the work done by the bureaucracy, we shall find the idea of the usefulness of official tutorship simply preposterous. And besides, what is the bureaucracy, whose wisdom and spirit are to move the body of the nation? Is it not just one fraction of the educated class, and nowadays precisely the very worst fraction? There are, of course, many brilliant exceptions, but the average officials are proverbial for their gross ignorance, corruption, and inefficiency. Thus to choose between autocracy and constitutional government is to choose between entrusting the affairs of the country to the worst section of the educated class uncontrolled, or entrusting them to the picked men under the permanent control of the press, public opinion, the whole body of citizens.

It is hardly possible, even for a foreigner, to hesitate as to which side to take. But for a Russian, who knows what the difference really is, the very idea that such a dilemma may be seriously considered is an absurdity.

As long as serfdom was preserved, it might be urged that, whether made up from the best or worst elements, autocracy was the only form of government that was possible in Russia. Only an iron military despotism could keep law and order in a community composed of a handful of masters and millions of slaves, who were ready to fly at their throats at the first opportunity. The Decembrists, who attacked autocracy, arms in hand, in 1825, were right in planning a simultaneous liberation of the people from their masters, and of the country from the Tzars.

With the abolition of serfdom in 1861, the autocracy lost its *raison d'être*. Russia became a European country in her internal structure. She could be governed by European methods, and by this time the intellectual forces outside the official world were incomparably superior to those represented by bureaucracy. Alexander II. was successful in his reforms only because, and in so far as, he was willing to utilize forces outside the official world.

The country had outgrown the bureaucratic phase of progress, and would have walked much better on its own legs than on the straps held by the Government.

But its legs were fettered and it had to break the chains first. The attempt to do it by bombs and dynamite was made, as we have seen, at the close of the reign of Alexander II., when the exceedingly rapid internal progress in every direction made the deadly stagnancy of the political forms unendurable. The attempt failed, and autocracy under Alexander III. became more stringent than before. The internal culture, and with it the capacity and the desire for freedom, grew uninterruptedly and as rapidly as in the previous period. It was natural that under such conditions the form of the struggle should be changed. After the failure of the efforts resulting from the acuteness of the discontent, people began to think of utilizing the widespread disaffection.

The later phase of the revolutionary movement is characterized by its great moderation. No single party has been formed that could speak for the whole body of revolutionists as the *Narodnaia Volia* did in 1879-83.

But all the more suggestive is the fact that all sections, large and small, into which the party divided, came to exactly the same conclusions and repeated the same demands almost word for word.

The secret printing offices never stopped their work in Russia. Over a score of them were discovered in the course of 1883-90, the whole staff being sent to the mines or to the Arctic region. But this dismemberment never prevented their being reconstructed over and over again. At any given moment two or three printing offices were at work in some corner of the capital or in some big provincial town. In 1883-4 there were six such printing offices, two in the capital and four in the provinces. Each of these printing presses was the centre of some independent organization, sometimes local, sometimes general, and its publications give a very clear idea of the prevailing tendencies of the revolutionary party.

Now if we look in their different publications we find that the dominant note in them is the desire to broaden the basis of the movement, and that they appeal to the whole of discontented educated Russia. Thus the St. Petersburg printing press, which was discovered by the police in 1883, published the speech of the well-known barrister, Plevako, suppressed by the Government on account of its constitutional demands, but which contained no revolutionary matter. In the December of the same year a body of Moderate Liberals drew up a statement of their views and demands, which did not go beyond a chamber of deputies, with advisory powers only. The printing press of the revolutionists took the risk of publishing this piece of milk and water liberalism, and in the next issue of the *Narodnaia Volia*, the editors, although expressing their disagreement with the proclamation, spoke of it sympathetically as an important sign of the times.

In 1884 another printing office, founded by Sophia Sladkova, published the manifesto of the "League of Youth," which, although socialistic in its ultimate objects, declares itself in favour of constitutional reform and educational work as the means by which the object will be obtained. Similar is the tone of the pamphlet issued by the Kharkov Printing Office, founded by the agrarian Socialists (the Land Partition party). It was discovered, owing to the treason of a certain Shkriaba, who was in consequence promptly killed by the revolutionists. But the idea of a peaceful Socialist propaganda was taken up by the Moscow Printing Press, which issued an organ called *The Union*, and a number of socialist pamphlets. The printing offices founded by the remnant of the *Narodnaia Volia* party at the two extremities of the Empire—in Dorpat and in Rostov, upon the Don, emphasize still more this turning point in the policy of the revolutionary party. The following year, 1885, the movement became more accentuated, as the *Labour Gazette* shows, issued by the new secret printing office of St. Petersburg, and the *Narodnaia Volia*, which had to found a new printing press in Taganrog.

One more illustration to prove the generality of their current of ideas. In 1887 the Russian revolutionists resolved to have a paper edited in St. Petersburg, but published in Switzerland, in order to avoid the danger of detection. The scheme could not be successful, as no paper could stand such a long distance between the editorial and the printing department. Two numbers only of this paper, bearing the characteristic name of *Self-government*, appeared in Geneva; the first contained the programme of the paper and a number of letters from political refugees, representing almost all sections and divisions of this rather disunited body. There is in this paper a letter from Debagory Mokrievich, one of the most active and gifted among Southern revolutionists. There are also letters from Dobrovolsky, a former medical officer of the Zemstvos, who sacrificed his situation and a good career for the sake of Socialist propaganda, and who had after his acquittal to escape abroad to avoid exile to Siberia; the famous Vera Zassulich, Axelrod, and the brilliant and erudite Plekhanov, who stand for the Russian social democracy; Professor Dragomanov, the leader of the Southern Russian Nationalist and Socialist movement, and many others, including the author of this book. A motley crowd it may seem, but not to one who peruses the statement of their views, because they are all agreed and united upon the point of a moderate political reform as the immediate step to be taken to give the Russian people the means of developing peacefully and organically in the direction best suited to them.

But under this broad and general movement we notice an undercurrent of extreme tendencies, which remind us of the epoch of the terrorist struggle. The dynamite manufacturers are not so numerous as the printing offices, but they are there nevertheless to repeat their *memento mori* to the tyranny above.

As early as the autumn of 1884 a dynamite workshop was discovered in the province of the Cossacks of the Don (Lugansky). In 1886 another dynamite factory was at work in the same region. In 1887 an attempt was made to blow up the Tzar with dynamite bombs on the anniversary of the death of Alexander II., when the Tzar goes invariably to a funeral mass at the Cathedral of SS. Peter and Paul. Though ably conceived, the bombs being made in the shape of books, which the conspirators held under their armpits, the attempt failed. The missiles were so badly manufactured that they did not explode. But very soon a marked improvement was made in that direction. In Zurich a company of revolutionists brought the manufacture of bombs almost to perfection, reducing them to the size of a watch without any decrease in their deadly effect. By an unexpected explosion the chief inventor and maker, Brinstein (Demba), was killed and his colleague wounded. Arrests followed, and the factory was moved to Paris. From there a girl, Sophia Gunsburg, was sent over to Russia to introduce the perfected weapon. But she was arrested, and the plan had to be abandoned because the French police arrested the conspirators before anything could be done. A new dynamite factory was founded in 1891 by Manzevich, who was arrested and locked up for life in Schlusselbourg by "administrative orders." But the seeds of dynamite seems to have taken root in the soil, for its deadly fruit reappears on the surface over and over again. Dynamite factories can no longer be extirpated, and every now and then the police discover proofs of fresh attempts to make practical use of the stuff manufactured by them. The attempt to blow up the Tzar at the Smolensk military manœuvre in 1893 seems to have been much more serious than that of March 13th, 1887. The new number of *Narodnaia Volia*, which appeared in 1893, gave expression to this newly awakened spirit of revenge and retaliation; the spectre of terrorism reappears in it once again.

One often hears worthy persons with sympathetic pity say, that of the hundred and ten millions of inhabitants of Russia, the Tzar is the one whose life is perhaps the least enviable. There is something in that, undoubtedly. The sort of existence which Alexander II. prepared for himself during the last years of his reign, and Alexander III. throughout the whole of his, was by no means to be envied. This one must admit. But there is no denying that fortune was particularly propitious to the young heir of their greatness, in creating for him an altogether exceptional position, which any ruler might envy. Together with uncontested power, he received the opportunity of accomplishing great things for the benefit of his country, with very little trouble to himself, and without the slightest damage to what is called the imperial prestige, or, to speak more correctly, the petty conceit and vanity of royalty. The unfortunate Alexander II., who started with the great idea of reform, had not the courage to carry out his mission to its logical end. He stopped short after a few years and began to undo his own work. When, after fifteen years of relentless reaction, the Russian people lost all patience and all confidence in him, and the Terrorist outbreaks occurred, to have recognized his error and to have granted a constitution then would have been to yield to reason supported by force. His pride rebelled against such a course, and he tried to put down the opposition, violent and peaceful alike, with the result that everybody knows. Alexander III. had a terrible legacy of blood and revenge left to him; and for him to abandon the path of reaction, and brave the suspicion that he was influenced by fear, would have required an unusual amount of moral courage, even supposing he had had sufficient independence and energy of mind to strike out a way for himself.

The position of the present Tzar is altogether different. He has no old account to settle, no obligation to exhibit fortitude. His hands are free, and will remain so for some time. No one could suspect that any concessions on his part were due to anything but his own spontaneous impulse to do good to his country. And at the time of his accession to the throne he was the object of that general feeling of goodwill and conciliatory forbearance, which facilitates the most difficult measures in practical politics, and goes half-way to ensure their success.

Before his accession to the throne, Nicholas II. attracted remarkably little attention. He was so young. The Tzar, Alexander III., seemed to be in excellent health, and the question of succession seemed so remote. People hardly distinguished the Tzarevich from the host of shadowy grand dukes. No opinions, no leanings to one party or another were attributed to him. The circle in which he moved was quite colourless. Of the little body of young aristocrats who surrounded him in the quality of friends, not a single one was mentioned as a man of ability. In fact, they effaced themselves later on, leaving the young Tzar in the hands of his father's old advisers. And the Tzarevich himself did not strike anyone as a man in any way brilliant. His former teachers were not over enthusiastic about his natural gifts. Those who had the opportunity of meeting him at his first public appearance, i e. during his journey round the globe, through Egypt, India, Japan, and Siberia, and at different courts of Europe, were similarly impressed by him. A very haughty, rough demeanour to inferiors and those who ministered to his comforts distinguished him unfavourably from the members of other reigning houses, with whom personal courtesy is a common characteristic. Love of pleasure, and an amazing ignorance, may be added as another trait in this vague sketch. On seeing the distillation of sea-water on a steamer, he asked what was the object of the operation, and wanted to know whether the sea-salt would not evaporate, and pass into the refrigerator with the steam.

As chairman of the famine relief committee, in 1891, he did nothing deserving of any attention, and showed a marked aversion to public business, i.e. to the reading and signing of reports and other official documents—a trait which was rather promising than otherwise in the son of his father. But it is impossible to make any forecast about a ruler from what he has been as a ruler in *spe*, especially in Russia, where it is not only improper, but even a little risky for the heir to the throne to make himself conspicuous, and assert his individuality in any way. It is well known that to dispel the suspicions of his father, Alexander II., as heir apparent, had to assume up to the age of thirty-six a mask of conservative apathy and indifference to public affairs which he was far from feeling at that time. When later on, his own heir, the future Alexander III., showed in private his leaning toward Slavophilism, his purely personal relations with Aksakov were interpreted as political conspiracies. He was put under police *surveillance*, and his private correspondence was opened like that of a suspected Nihilist.

We may assume that for the present Tzar this policy of self-effacement can have cost no great effort, for it does not seem that he had much individuality to show, either in views or character. But the Russian public was, so far, unaware of the fact, or, if aware of it, indifferent on the subject. He was young, and the faith which men have in the generosity, unselfishness, and purity of youth, went to swell that wave of hope and warm confidence which greeted his accession to the throne. In one night Russia seemed to have grown young again.

The pent-up rancour and spirit of revenge which had been accumulated by the horrors of the past reign, the fierce and gloomy despair which was ready to break out in new deeds of blood, were suddenly transformed into joyful, confident hope—as a gathering storm is sometimes dissolved into a warm, beneficent summer rain. The extreme, or, to be more accurate, the more consistent and logical section of the opposition, upon whom the experience of the past was not lost, knew very well that it was childish to expect any concession without corresponding pressure. Yet even they looked hopefully into the future, expecting that the new government of so young a man being weaker than the preceding one, the amount of pressure necessary to produce the desired effect might be smaller and less violent. But with the bulk of society this flood of hopefulness came from a rush of sudden faith in the personality of the young Tzar, in his good intentions, his true, genuine love for his country. It is interesting that it was the *Novoe Vremya*—the most cynically reactionary and wide-awake of all Russian papers—that expressed most forcibly the dominant feeling of the moment.

"Russia looks hopefully upon her new sovereign. He is young—but youth is not a defect. Youth is generous, and so little is needed to give happiness to our long-suffering country."

In fact, very little would have pacified Russia. The more far-sighted section of the opposition put forward the demand for a constitution, such as we see in the rest of Europe. But the bulk of the Liberal party did not ask even that little. From the utterances of the Liberal press, and from the statements of the representative bodies which had the courage to express their opinions, and from other information and indications, we may gather that the bulk of the Liberal opposition has been, and is willing to compromise upon a Chamber of Deputies, with powers of advising only.

To show how exceedingly (one may say how excessively) moderate such a demand is, it is enough to mention that there is, and has been for half a century, a body which had such a counselling and deliberative voice in legislation—the so-called Council of State (Gossudarstvenny Sovet), which transacts all the legislative work. The Ministers smuggle in some laws of their own making, by means of circulars having the force of law, or by their obligatory "comments" on laws which sometimes are in flagrant contradiction to the law commented upon. But as a rule, every project of new law, after being drawn up in the corresponding ministerial department, is laid before the Council of the State, which discusses it, proposes amendments, and passes a resolution for or against the project, the Tzar having the option of sanctioning the view of the majority or the minority, after which the project becomes law.

The crazy Paul I. alone wrote his silly laws himself, without consulting anyone. All the other Tzars had the good sense never to make full use of their discretionary power of legislating. The Tzars do sometimes initiate new laws by giving an order to the corresponding Minister, but before being promulgated, they invariably pass through some deliberative body—the Council of the State—Gossudarstvenny Sovet—as a general rule, or the Council of Ministers in exceptional cases.

An assembly of representatives of the people, with powers of advising, would simply mean a change in the *personnel* of the State Council. Instead of being nominated by the Tzar, these experts in legislative matters would be sent in by the nation. One may doubt whether such a reform would be sufficient to guarantee to the nation the management of her own affairs. But it was not for the autocrat to resent such an insufficiency; and the smaller the demands, the less reason there was to anticipate resistance. It is so pleasant to dream of easy, heaven-sent gifts—and for two months Russian society revelled in rosy dreams.

Every act of the new Tzar was watched with breathless attention, and the most favourable interpretation was put on it. There was a tacit conspiracy of praise and encouragement. The Russian people condoned the young Tzar's first manifesto, announcing his accession to the throne of his forefathers, and declaring that Russia's greatness depended upon implicit devotion and obedience to him. This was rather presumptuous on the part of a young man of twenty-six, but the sponge was passed over it, people accepting such utterances as a tribute to routine, and waiting with the same hopeful, benevolent indulgence for some sign to come.

Two insignificant concessions made in the first days of the new reign, served to keep alive hopes which were the sickly offspring of lazy optimism. In the controversy between the Poles and the Governor-General, the coarse cavalry sergeant Gurko, the young Tzar sided with the former. He condescended to permit his Polish subjects to take their oath of allegiance in their own language, and not in the official Russian, which they did not understand. The offended general sent in his resignation, which was accepted. For this little concession the Poles received Gurko's successor, General Orzevsky, with something like an ovation, and on December 6th, the Tzar's name day, Warsaw was brilliantly illuminated by the Poles without any compulsion on the part of the police. No Tzar had ever been so honoured by the citizens of the proud Polish capital. Certainly Nicholas II. could not complain of lack of sympathetic encouragement.

The Finnish controversy was somewhat more serious, and the young Tzar appears in it in a favourable light, showing a capacity for listening to reason and admitting his errors, which is very uncommon in kings and emperors.

In the first manifesto of the Tzar, announcing his assumption of the crown of the Russian Empire and of the grand Duchy of Finland, the latter was mentioned as "indissolubly united" to Russia, whilst the Finns consider their country to be quite apart from the rest of the Empire, the two crowns only being united on the same head. Besides, as constitutional sovereigns of Finland, the Tzars, at their accession to the throne, were expected to sign the promise to adhere to the constitution of the Grand Duchy, after which the Finns took their oath of allegiance. Nicholas II. omitted to comply with this rule, which greatly alarmed the Finns. In view of the attacks upon their constitution, which had marked the last year of the preceding reign, they very rightly considered the conduct of the young Tzar as a very bad omen, and resolved to make a stand for their ancient liberties. By common agreement they put off taking the oath of allegiance, sending their official representative, the Secretary of State, General Denn, to Livadia to remonstrate with the new Tzar, and to obtain his signature to the promissory act. For seven days Finland was in a state of great suspense, until a telegram was received from General Denn, announcing that the young Tzar had signed the promissory act, and ordered the error of his first manifesto to be set right, after which the oath of allegiance was taken all over the country.

As a set-off against these two facts, the dismissal of General Gurko and the acceptance of Finnish remonstrances, which were to the young Tzar's credit, there were a number of other facts which told in the opposite direction. Stringent decrees against the Stundists and the Jews were issued a few days after the manifesto by which Nicholas II. announced his accession to the throne. The censorship was as relentless as before, and police raids, with their invariable sequel—arrests, imprisonment, exile —were more fierce and indiscriminating than ever. The balance between debit and credit was much against the prospects of the new reign. But the public would not make any such balance. All that was bad was put down to officials, whilst all that showed a shadow of progressive tendencies was hailed as a ray of sunshine on a gloomy day.

The grounds for such enthusiasm were so exceedingly poor that one cannot help suspecting that it was not altogether genuine. Worthy persons hoped that the young Tzar could be carried away by dint of praises. The taste for popularity grows, and he might wish to gain more of the praise which had been so profusely lavished upon him on credit, and might come to believe himself to be what men assured him that he was. Nurses sometimes use this trick with naughty children, telling them they are good boys, till they get them to behave as such.

But this simple-minded device did not prove successful in its new application. The young Tzar either took the praises literally as his desert, or was naturally destitute of those imaginative qualities which would have allowed him to develop the taste for popularity.

On his return from Livadia he seemed to be under good control, never committing any act that might "cause a dangerous excitement of public opinion," to use the favourite expression of the censorship. The old gang gained complete possession of him, and the internal policy seemed gradually to slide into the old groove. All ministers of the former reign were kept in office except Krivoshein, who lost his post through his clumsiness in the embezzlement of public money. Durnavo, the minister of the interior, got so far reassured that, at a private interview with the editors of the chief papers of the capital, he was bold enough to affirm that no change whatever was to be expected, and that everything would remain exactly as before. So it seemed in fact. But the young Tzar did not show his hand, and people waited and hoped for a sign.

The marriage of the young Tzar with Princess Alix had to take place within a few weeks. People waited anxiously for this event, because it was bound to draw the Tzar from his reserve. The manifestoes which are invariably issued on such occasions, though essentially non-political, always show the political tendency prevailing in high quarters. The golden document, the cornucopia of graces, came in due time. The foreign press, through inertia following the earlier impulse, greeted it as an act of supreme clemency such as Russia had not seen for half a century. But the Russians themselves knew better. With the best wishes they could not keep up any illusion as to the nature of this manifesto. The peasants got their usual condonation of arrears, that could not be collected, and old debts to the state, which could not be recovered. Otherwise the manifesto was the stingiest and meanest thing of the kind that had been issued for a long time. Thieves, burglars, depredators of public funds were the only people for whom the young sovereign kept a corner in his heart. As to offences committed as a protest against the prevailing oppression or intolerance, they were either overlooked and ignored or dealt with in such a spirit of petty rancour and spitefulness as fully to confirm the opinion of some English papers, that this document was something altogether exceptional. Not a ray of hope for the many hundreds of men who were suffering for their religious opinions. Not a word as to offenders against the press regulations, who are everywhere the first to benefit by any amnesty.

The Poles, the traditional victims of Russian Tzars, were remembered indeed, but only to be made the object of a practical joke. Those who had taken part in the insurrection of thirty-two years ago, who still remained in Siberia, were allowed to return and settle *everywhere*, except in those places where the Minister of the Interior should consider their presence dangerous to public order. This meant, of course, Poland. Thus it was with the Minister of the Interior that the decision as to the amnesty granted to Poles finally rested.

As regards political offenders in general, only one category of "criminals" received a real amnesty;—those who fell under the Article 447 of the Penal Code. But if we look up this Article, we find that it refers to offences which it is a shame to consider offences at all, namely, the "offences against the portraits, statues, or busts of the Tzar or members of his family," i.e. damaging or destroying the sacred images; and also to "disrespectful and offensive words" about the Emperor or his family, "pronounced without any intention to excite disrespect to the sacred person of the Emperor," i.e. in a state of drunkenness or in a moment of excitement, when some people will find relief in senseless swearing.

The real political offenders are dealt with in a manner which is both insulting and cowardly.

Nothing is given without some mean subterfuge allowing the Administration to take it away. The lightening of the penalties of prisoners or Siberian exiles is made conditional upon their good behaviour, which means that they are put entirely at the mercy of the Minister and the Administration. With reference to political offenders, bad behaviour means faithfulness to the principles for which they are suffering—often simply a dignified attitude of reserve.

This mean-spirited cautiousness is still more apparent in the paragraph referring to political refugees. They are graciously allowed to petition the Minister of the Interior for permission to return to their country, on condition of their being willing " to atone for their past crimes by sincere repentance and fidelity to the throne." This does not exactly sound like clemency or grace. The right of recanting has never been denied to political offenders, and the renegades have at all times been received with open arms by the Government.

I have only to remind the reader of the case of Lev Tikhomirov, who, having repudiated his former creed, received free pardon from Alexander III., although he was a member of the committee which condemned

Alexander II. to death. Several men of less prominence, who have followed Tikhomirov's example, have been all pardoned and allowed to return. And here again we see, in the manifesto of Nicholas II., a clause which elevates the bureaucracy to a higher place than it held before. With regard to refugees as with regard to the Poles, the Minister of the Interior is made the dispenser and controller of the Tzar's privilege of mercy, which was never officially relinquished by any of Nicholas II.'s predecessors.

According to the strict terms of the manifesto, the Minister of the Interior has the option of submitting to the Tzar or not the petitions of the repentant refugees; he is "permitted" to accept such petitions, and pass them on in due course. Now what is "permitted," is, *ipso facto*, optional.

Of course, we do not mean in the least to blame the young Tzar for any obstacle he puts in the way of renegades. We mention this point only as another indication of the greater ascendancy of bureaucracy, to which the new Tzar shows himself so yielding.

One more curious detail. The Minister of the Interior has not full discretion in the matter;

the manifesto puts one restriction on him : he is prohibited from forwarding to the Tzar the petitions of refugees whose offences fall under Section 249 of the Penal Code.

One would think that these must be the tzaricides, and worse. But if we look into the Article in question, we find that it practically covers the whole ground of political offences.

Here is the famous Article, which has been referred to constantly for the last fifteen years. "For rebellion against the supreme authority, i.e. for an open insurrection and conspiracy against the Tzar and the State, as well as for the intention to overthrow the Government in the whole Empire, or a part thereof, or to *change the system of government* . . . . all the promoters, inciters, associates, and abettors, are subjected to the penalty of death; those who knew of the criminal preparations, and having the possibility of informing the authorities of them, have not done so, being liable to the same penalty."

It is clear that any participation in revolutionary conspiracy is covered by this paragraph; and in fact, since 1879, i.e. since the Revolutionary Party included in its programme the overthrow of autocracy, all revolutionists have been indicted on the strength of this terrible 249th paragraph. All were declared by the Imperial Prosecutor worthy of death, and any mitigation of their penalties was represented as a peculiar act of mercy.

The mention of this paragraph in the manifesto makes it a piece of buffoonery, and we are led to conclude that either the young Tzar has been fooling the simple public, or that he has been fooled, and has put his name to the first great document of his reign without taking the trouble to understand clearly what was behind its clumsy paragraphs.

If the section referring to political offenders is interesting as throwing a sidelight on the Tzar's personal character, the section dealing with the exile system has a wider bearing, because it foreshadows a whole system of policy.

No interior peace, no justice, no civil guarantees, no abatement of bureaucratic tyranny is to be thought of as long as the system of exile by administrative order is maintained.

Now there is no doubt possible as to that. Administrative exile is mentioned throughout the manifesto as something unquestionable, forming an integral part of the system of government.

The victims of administrative tyranny have fared even worse than the victims of judicial subserviency. Political offenders who have been tried and sentenced, have had their penalties commuted, except in cases where the administration chose to interfere. Administrative exiles had no alleviation of their suffering, except in the cases where the Administration was pleased to pronounce in their favour.

After the publication of the manifesto of January 26th, any unprejudiced man could see clearly that there was nothing to be hoped for from the new reign. But the Russian public has, to an unusual degree, the capacity of hoping against hope, and the great solemnities of the Court, such as marriages, coronations, and the like, afford an opportunity for exhibiting this amiable characteristic.

Disappointed by the marriage manifesto, they would have fixed their hopes upon the coronation; but here something unexpected occurred; the young Tzar stepped himself from the clouds of the bureaucratic Olympus, and made a statement so plain and unequivocal as to render any further illusion impossible.

Our great satirist, Shtchedrin, makes one of his heroes regret that he is not a dumb animal, an ox for example, because no man can feel safe in Russia, no matter what one says ; any speech may be misinterpreted by spies, and lead the speaker into trouble. Whilst if one were merely bellowing, what could the cleverest spies make out of it ?

For the Tzar, too, it would be much pleasanter if his subjects could only bellow. As they have the gift of speech without the right to use it—or as Mme. Novikov puts it, as they enjoy perfect freedom of opinion without the right of giving it utterance—very untoward incidents will sometimes happen. They are expected to speak, and must speak on certain great occasions, because a solemn ceremony in dumb show would be too monotonous. Naturally enough, objectionable opinions will find articulate expression every now and then. That is just what the young Tzar learnt to his cost.

In reply to the first manifesto of the Tzar, the one announcing his accession to the throne and his future marriage, the different provinces of the Empire sent in deputations to the capital to congratulate him on these two events. Several Zemstvos took this opportunity to express to the young sovereign the true feelings and wishes of the country. These were the

Zemstvos of Tver, Tchernigov, etc. To show the nature of these extremely moderate demands, it will suffice to quote the address of the Zemstvo of Tver, which was the most outspoken and dignified. Here it is, in a slightly condensed form :—

"Your Majesty,—In the solemn days of the beginning of your service to the Russian people, the Zemstvo of Tver greets you with the greeting of faithful subjects. . . . Together with the whole of Russia we have listened to the significant words by which your Majesty has announced your accession to the Russian throne. We are filled with gratitude for your resolution to devote yourself to the happiness of your people, and we hope for the success of the great task you have put before yourself. We trust that the voice of the people's needs will be always heard on the height of the throne. We trust that our prosperity will grow together with the unflinching obedience to law both on the part of the people and of the Administration ; because the law, expressing in Russia the will of the monarch, must stand above the changeful views of the individual agents of that supreme authority. We earnestly hope that the rights of individual citizens as well as of the corporations will be protected. We expect, Sire, that public bodies and corporations will have the possibility and the right of expressing their opinions upon questions concerning them, in order that the monarch may be able to hear the views and the desires not only of the Administration, but of the Russian people as well. We believe that in a closer intercourse with the representatives of all classes of the Russian people, who are equally devoted to the throne and the country, the authority of your Majesty will find a new source of strength and a pledge of success for your generous intentions."

The address of the Zemstvo of Tula is, we will not say more moderate, because it is difficult to be more moderate than the representatives of Tver, but it is couched in terms so obsequious that only the sensitive ear of a Russian can detect in it the spark of opposition. After reiterated expressions of devotion and loyalty, the Zemstvo of Tula is bold enough to say:—

"As men standing very close to the people, we have a strong belief that local needs can be satisfied only through representatives of local interests, and we beg our Tzar to have confidence in us, which is a necessary condition for fruitful service to the country. We beg for a free access for the voices of the Zemstvos to the throne."

These quotations are fair samples from the bulk. Certainly no despot has been approached by his dissatisfied subjects in so conciliatory a spirit.

Before submitting these addresses to the Emperor, all the deputations had to hand them over to the Minister of the Interior, who had to decide whether they were fit to be presented to the Tzar. The addresses of the liberal Zemstvos were declared unfit for presentation, and the deputies of the Zemstvo of Tver were deprived by the Minister of the happiness of appearing before the Tzar. Of course the Tzar was informed of the transgression of the liberal Zemstvos, and had time to think it over and prepare his reply, which we are therefore bound to consider as the deliberate statement of his views. This reply is well known to the whole of the English public, upon whom it fell like a bucket of cold water. After expressing his sovereign pleasure at the feelings of loyalty and boundless devotion to him expressed by the deputies, the Tzar said:—

"I rejoice to see gathered here representatives of all estates of the realm, who have come to give expression to their sentiments of loyal allegiance. I believe in the sincerity of these feelings, which have been those of every Russian from time immemorial. But it has come to my knowledge that latterly, in some meetings of the Zemstvos, voices have made themselves heard from people who have allowed themselves to be carried away by foolish fancies about the participation of representatives of the Zemstvos in the general administration of the internal affairs of the State. Let all know that I devote all my strength to the good of my people, but that I shall uphold the principle of autocracy as firmly and unflinchingly as did my ever-lamented father."

The official papers reported that the speech was received with enthusiastic cheers. But it was not so. An eye-witness tells us that there was much cheering at the opening of the speech, but its concluding words were received in dead silence. On the next day at the thanksgiving Mass, which had been arranged beforehand, out of 600 delegates only 30 were present. Those of the correspondents of the foreign press, German and English, who write from the spot, have all reported that the Tzar's speech caused great dissatisfaction. Even the Russian papers, gagged as they are by the censorship, bear unmistakable signs of a revulsion of public opinion in Russia. It could not be otherwise; for, apart from its substance, the form alone of the Tzar's speech was bound to produce the worst possible impression. Politeness is the supreme law among educated people, no matter what their station, and people could not help being hurt by the rudeness of a man, who, whatever else he may be, is a mere stripling of no experience compared with the elderly people, marshals of nobility, ancient judges, and presidents of the Zemstvos, whom he chose to treat as if they were schoolboys.

Politically, the speech of December 20th marks an epoch in the history of our opposition movement. Hitherto the Government had pretended that only outlaws, madcaps of revolutionists, socialists, and other disreputable persons were clamouring for the reform of our political system. Nicholas II. was the first to confess publicly that the country, through its accredited representatives, was asking him for constitutional reform, and he, the Tzar, was refusing to accede to its demands, and meant to refuse as long as he could.

The internal policy of the new reign, which had been up to then a blank, was defined by the Tzar's speech to the Zemstvos: it would be preposterous to say once for all, but certainly for some time to come. Nicholas II. has pledged himself to the policy of blind reaction, and it will be much more difficult to retrace his steps than to start off in the right direction. The new reign is intended to be a slavish imitation of the preceding one. The same tendencies, the same men, the same methods. The new Tzar seems utterly to lack all ambition to do anything on his own account, as every other Tzar has tried to do—at the beginning of his reign at least. Nicholas II., although in all the ardour of youth, is satisfied with following the beaten track of officialism.

It is the story of King Log and King Stork, only that the order of succession has been inverted. King Stork preceded King Log. But unfortunately the neutrality of the present Tzar does not mean immunity from oppression. It means simply an unbridled rule of the bureaucracy, which is now freed from the very semblance of control. Under Alexander III. bureaucratic despotism was hidden in the shade of autocracy; now we shall have the frank supremacy of bureaucracy keeping in its shade a Tzar as a figure-head.

The reign of Alexander III. was a test of autocratic principle. That of Nicholas II. promises to show what bureaucracy is like when left to its own impulses.

The reaction, which under Alexander II. was the result of inconsistency and weakness of purpose, and under Alexander III. was taken by simple-minded people as the consequence of the revenge wreaked on the nation for the humiliating hesitations caused by the attacks of the revolutionists—this reaction comes now as the natural policy of an autocracy which has become too poor-spirited to start on any new line, no matter how advantageous.

Relentless, implacable hostility towards the whole of enlightened, educated Russia, and patriarchal benevolence toward the peasants, such is the policy of the new Tzar. But in a bureaucratic despotism, benevolence toward the peasants and solicitude for their interests can be manifested in one way only: by increasing the power of bureaucracy to interfere in the affairs of the peasants—that is, by their greater economical and political subjection to the officials.

We must always bear in mind that the tenderness of the "Little Father," the Tzar, to his "little children," the peasants, is not altogether disinterested. The peasants are the only section of the community that pay without asking what is done with the money. The middle and upper class will not submit to it. Knowing this, the autocrats act accordingly.

The Russian Tzars have had but one expedient for staving off as long as possible the necessity of appealing for support to the country —to put the screw upon the peasants. And in order to squeeze from the peasants as much as possible, the Government naturally tries to make their work as fruitful as possible; and for the past twenty-five years the Russian Government has been engaged in solving the interesting economic problem of how to make the peasant's labour as productive as that of a free man, while it deprives him of the fruits of his labour as completely as if he were a slave. This economic puzzle has been solved by the introduction of a kind of collective slavery of the peasants to the State. For whilst the individual is left just enough freedom to make him dependent upon his own resources, the State assigns to itself the better half of his income.

But each individual peasant knows that not half but the whole of his income may go, and that he may be left a beggar, unless he strains his wits and energies to the utmost and makes the best of his opportunities. Serfdom had no such effective stimulus; and the productivity of the national work has increased considerably, to the advantage of the State exclusively. Even with eighty million people working for it as serfs it has been unable to make both ends meet. But collective enslavement pushed beyond a certain limit leads unavoidably to individual enslavement.

After a time, economic pressure becomes insufficient to make labour highly productive. Something more stringent is demanded, and the Administration receives new powers of the patriarchal kind, and this time over individuals. The rod is re-introduced as an integral part of good government, and the peasants become gradually enslaved to the officials, just as they were earlier enslaved to the nobility.

The greater the expenses of the State the more "benevolent" the Tzars become toward the peasants, and the more solicitous that they shall not damage their own interests.

The paternal disposition of the young Tzar

means simply that he will go on turning the screw as long as it will stand it—a sad outlook for the peasants, and for the future of the dynasty as well.

But in our sceptical age men are suspicious of everything that may be called transcendental: transcendental virtue or vice, transcendental wisdom or foolishness. It seems incredible that a man in his senses should deliberately sit upon the safety-valve, knowing full well that an explosion must follow sooner or later, whilst he has in his hand a key to turn the tap and let off the dangerous steam.

Such dense self-destructive stupidity seems inconceivable. Hence the conclusion that for some reason or other the Tzar cannot re-mould the political organization of which he is the official head; for he would have certainly re-moulded it if he could.

The reasoning is perfectly correct in a sense. There must be something insuperable which stands in the way of the Tzar becoming the reformer of the political system of Russia. The question which Englishmen are asking is, What is it?

Fancy is the quickest and the most obliging

of our faculties, being always ready to fill in irritating gaps in our understanding; and fancy makes naturally for the sensational and striking.

Resting for a while its wondering gaze on the mightiest potentate of the world, who at the same time seems to be the most helpless of human beings, fancy very simply solves the riddle of the combination of power and weakness which it sees in him.

The Nihilists are urging the Tzar by their drastic arguments to liberal reforms, which seem desirable and likely to be beneficial all round. There must be in Russia at the Tzar's elbow another party as violent and extreme as the Nihilists, which pushes him in the opposite direction, and is, if pushed to the wall, ready to use the same means of intimidation as the Nihilists. Between the two fires the Tzar is unable to make his choice, and has no alternative but to tremble and maintain the *status quo*.

One constantly hears such surmises, in public meetings and in private, whenever Russian affairs are being discussed. These mysterious champions of reaction are called sometimes the Aristocratic Party, sometimes the Old Slavophils; but oftener, to enhance the mystery, they are left without any name. This is certainly the best plan. But we may do more; we may dismiss these bugbears altogether, for they do not exist at all. Every Russian of any education will say the same.

There is no Aristocratic Party in Russia, for the simple reason that in our country there is no aristocracy, in the scientific, historical sense of the word, the handful of people calling themselves aristocrats being only a class who have for several generations enjoyed certain privileges granted to them by the Crown at the expense of the people.

Of the Slavophils it is impossible to speak seriously. One smaller section of them, which is hardly represented nowadays, is a body of scholars and philosophers, who have not even that power which masterly word and thought give to men over their contemporaries. The other, bigger, section is entirely merged in the bureaucracy, representing in it certain ambitious and grasping tendencies of autocracy.

The only body of people in Russia that count in internal politics is the bureaucracy, the legions of officials who, although dependent individually and collectively upon the will of the Tzar, yet, owing to their number, and the impossibility of effective control, can thwart and nullify every order of their master, if they are so minded. But there is no cohesion, no feeling of solidarity among them. They will never openly rebel, never go on strike, or so much as show displeasure at any order given to them. Their resistance is passive, silent, submissive, but insuperable, because organic, as the result of certain constitutional qualities, traditions, and habits, which have become its second nature.

A Tzar trying to re-mould the state through bureaucracy is in the position of a man trying to lift up the stool upon which he is sitting. But there is nothing to prevent him from stepping upon the firm ground and finding a new point of support. The story of the greatest reform initiated by autocracy—the emancipation of the serfs—may serve as proof and illustration.

Nicholas I. was a sincere abolitionist, and as early as 1826 he made up his mind to emancipate the serfs. But being a blind adherent of the bureaucratic system, he entrusted the elaboration of an emancipation law to a commission of officials, who, as serf-owners, were naturally hostile to the measure. Whilst affecting complete obedience to the orders of the Tzar, they succeeded, by simple procrastination, in completely frustrating his intentions. For twenty whole years the commission was sitting, collecting materials, accumulating volumes in the archives, and not advancing one step; so that at the death of Nicholas I. the question was precisely at the same point as at his accession to the throne.

When Alexander II. resolved to carry out the same reform, the bureaucracy, as a body, was as hostile to it as the planters of the Southern States to the abolitionist plans of President Lincoln, and for the same reasons. But they never thought of disobeying the Tzar's orders, and they were not able to strangle the project in red tape, because this time the Tzar departed from the bureaucratic routine, and invited the co-operation of the vital forces of the country, the press, and public opinion, which rendered the carrying out of the reform possible, and would have improved it, and changed the face of the country, if he had not very soon after relapsed into his father's ways.

Suppose the Tzar had made up his mind to give Russia a constitution, there would have been no power to compel him to deviate from his resolution. The reactionary party at the Court, and the ministers who had thrown in their lot indissolubly with reaction, would have moved heaven and earth to bring all sorts of underhand pressure to bear upon him; they would have tried to frighten him with all sorts of imaginary dangers. But it would never occur to them to take any step actually forcing the Tzar's hand, or to so much as assume an attitude of open hostility or opposition.

The Shah of Persia and the Sultan of Turkey are more likely to meet with open opposition at their Court than the Tzar of Russia. Religious fanaticism can push people to rash steps, but courtiers' calculations cannot. Besides, as regards constitutional reform, the Court and the higher bureaucracy will be a house divided in itself. The light of culture has done its work, even in these benighted spheres, and there are nowadays many partisans of constitutional reform, even among the ministerial staff.

The Tzar, being only the head of a huge administrative machine, can do but little himself. But he could easily find willing assistants among the best men of the official class, as Alexander II. found for his early reforms.

There is no material obstacle to prevent the Tzar from starting constitutional reform, not a shadow of hidden force able to keep him in the ways of reaction. There can be no divided opinion upon this point among those who know anything about the Russian official world. The reader can accept this statement with perfect confidence. But we may as confidently affirm that if these material obstacles and imaginary dangers stood in the way, there would be more chance for the spontaneous resignation of autocratic power than there is now.

Bureaucracy has obtained a moral hold over the Tzar much more powerful than all the supposed intimidations on the part of the dark powers of reaction could ever have. He cannot escape from that bondage, because it is within himself. As the head of the bureaucracy, he has become imbued with the spirit, the habit of thought, and the views permeating that body. From an instrument at the service of the State, bureaucracy has become the embodiment of the State itself. The huge automaton has, in the course of generations, acquired a sort of fictitious vitality, and has cowed the mechanician, who dares not touch it for fear that the world will crumble into ruin with it.

The bigger and the more complicated the machinery of the State becomes, the less chance there is that any Tzar will touch it, and the greater, on the contrary, the temptation to keep at the head of the gigantic machine, in the vain hope of being able to direct its working.

The evil instincts and passions developed from very childhood in those whom men have been stupid enough to make the arbiters of the destinies of nations: pride, conceit, intolerance of criticism, and the enjoyment of their unapproachable, inaccessible superiority over all men living; all these instincts and passions are in themselves sufficiently strong obstacles to a despot's voluntarily relinquishing a part of his power. A man who has been always surrounded by flattery, who has been taught to consider himself as a superior being, destined by God, and the supposed blind devotion of the millions, to be the master, cannot be expected to become the champion of the rights of the people.

But, unfortunately, the intoxication of power is not due to evil instincts only. It is fed by good intentions. And if the progress of the humanitarian ideas of our age has so far influenced Russian autocracy as to make the absolutely selfish, epicurean despotism of the

Roman Cæsars or the Oriental Khans and Shahs impossible, it would mean that progress has only further diminished our chances of liberal reforms from above.

The more a man is conscious of his sincere desire to do good, the more he will stick to the power which he believes will give him the possibility of doing so.

As autocracy has undoubtedly rendered great services to the country in the past, it is very easy for one so disposed to persuade himself by a slight effort of imagination that it will do so in the present.

In one point, namely, in the aggrandizement of the State, autocracy really has the advantage over all other forms of government. A free Russia will be stronger in the interior. But no constitutional state can be so successful as autocracy in the work of conquest and annexation, because the vital forces and resources of the nation will be devoted to interior development. Foreign politics recede into the background with the growth of civil and political freedom, whilst it is the main prop of autocracies.

The official apologists for autocracy have advanced the plea that it is necessary for the preservation of the unity of the Empire. This is sheer nonsense, because the Russia of the Russians is a homogeneous organically united country, which cannot fall to pieces any more than the United States of America. Poland and Finland are not Russia. If, which is not likely, they prefer a separate existence as petty States to the advantage of a free political and economic union with a country like Russia, and secede, Russia will not be the loser by it. But for the further extension of the State in all directions, the maintenance of autocracy is undoubtedly necessary. And when will that process stop? Jingoism is insatiable.

The recent Japanese war has revealed the ambition of the Russian Government for supremacy in the far East, which had hitherto been concealed. It wants Manjuria and Corea, Port Arthur and what not for itself; to secure that end autocracy would not allow the Japanese to snatch the prey from her.

The Armenian scare has brought proof as evident of the covetousness of the Tzar's Russia in another direction. The Russian diplomatists would on no account consent to Armenian autonomy, because an independent Armenia, like the independent Bulgaria, would be a barrier to Russian extension; whilst an enslaved Armenia is sure to seek refuge from the horrors of Turkish rule under the sceptre of the White Tzar, and will, like the golden apple, fall sooner or later into his lap. This would give him the strategical key to dominion over the two seas, and transform both Asia Minor and Persia into Russian dependencies. And when the Russian frontier is "rounded" in those directions, will the "nationalist" ambition be satisfied? Will it not be too tempting to stretch the Russian frontier, and to extend the Russian markets to the strip of land now ruled by the Ameers, and then to leap over into the huge country of untold riches, defended only by seventy thousand soldiers? It will seem a defenceless prey to a commander of an army of four million men, which by that time will have grown to seven or eight.

Europe will never become Cossack, as Napoleon prophesied, the superiority of European culture being an insuperable obstacle to it. But the advantage is entirely on Russia's side in Asia, and there is no limit to her expansion in that direction. The late Count Von Moltke said that Russia may conquer, some day, the whole of Asia, except

India. But his book was written some fifty years ago, when the enormous military advantages of countries which have introduced universal conscription could not be foreseen. Would he maintain the same exception now? Or, what is more to the point, would Russian "Jingoes" necessarily endorse it?

Now there is so much of the brutal instincts of savages left in the common herd of men, that thousands of them will sell their birthright of freedom for the sake of the purely platonic enjoyment of the idea that their country is trampling on other nations, and crushing them to dust. That is why autocrats seek to surround themselves with the glamour of military glory.

One can well realize that those who stand at the head of the State, and are themselves the chief actors in this Jingoistic *épopée*, may have their heads turned by its gorgeous vistas, and consider it not only permissible, but praiseworthy, to deny the people their freedom for the sake of such a "grand" future.

And that is not all there is to sustain autocratic obstinacy. There is the fiction of the all-powerful ruler, standing as a tribune of the people, above class interests and class jealousies, and able to be the benefactor and protector of the masses. This fiction has been exploded scores of times, and never so thoroughly as during the past reign. Yet it recurs over and over again in the highest quarters, as with the lowest stratas of the rural population, because the ignorance of the realities of our political life prevailing at the Imperial Court is as dense and impenetrable as that which obtains in the most benighted sections of our peasantry. There is the narrow and one-sided criticism of parliamentary institutions, the exaggerations of their small drawbacks, and the overlooking of their great advantages; a criticism to which those systems are particularly open now in the epoch of social struggle, the most advanced countries being on the eve of the creation of new social and political life. The entanglement of the French parliamentary system, the Panama scandals, as well as the senseless dynamite outrages, are all fuel to the autocratic fire.

If a Mr. Stead is ready to sum up his defence of autocracy in Russia by telling us that the constitutional *régime* is after all as bad as autocracy, why should we expect a Nicholas II. to be less foolish and more discriminating?

. And the broader, the more enlightened, and

truly democratic conceptions of the sovereign's duties and of people's rights—where are they to come from?

In the palmy days of autocracy, when it had an absolute unshakable confidence in its own stability, new ideas had a freer access to the court. The Empress Catherine II. entrusted the education of the future Alexander I. to the republican La Harpe, and Nicholas I. called to the same office the humanitarian poet, Joukovsky, who was one of the leading men of his time. But such things are not possible nowadays. Autocracy has been cowed, and become suspicious and cautious. Men holding the same positions among their contemporaries as La Harpe and Joukovsky will not be allowed to come within gunshot of the court.

All that penetrates into the secret precincts of the Imperial Court—men, books, newspapers alike—are carefully tested, and the Tzar, grand dukes and duchesses, up to the most distant branches, are kept under a supervision much more strict than the most "dangerous" class of citizens.

Acting systematically and uninterruptedly for at least two score of years, that sort of "natural selection" has debased the intellectual standard of our highest circles to a degree that is inconceivable to ordinary mortals. At the same time, the race of the Romanovs, like all the other families that are placed in similar conditions, has not been improving physically and mentally. On the contrary, there is a marked degeneration in this respect, as with the Bourbon dynasty in France, or in Spain, or Italy. This is an unpleasant subject, which cannot be dealt with in detail in a book intended for the general public. But it is an evident fact which may be alluded to cursorily.

There is little chance of another Peter the Great coming upon the Russian throne, to make up for the lost time, and once again bring Russian political institutions into harmony with those of the European West.

Nature has wonderful caprices, and a happy accident may belie all these forecasts. But it is most unlikely that such a happy exception should be ever presented by the legitimate heir to the throne, who naturally has the least chance of becoming such an exception. And if among the other members of the Imperial family, men or women, there should be one so especially favoured by nature and circumstances as to escape being cast in the common mould, the only way for making such a happy anomaly of any use would be through a palace revolution, which would dethrone the elder branch of the dynasty, putting in its place a younger one. This would be the easiest and quietest solution of the Russian political crisis, and one cannot say that it is impossible. Otherwise Russia has nothing to hope for except through revolutionary methods; the active revolution in any form or shape, or the threat of one which would compel the autocracy to lay down its arms.

It is very unfortunate that such a course should be forced upon us. The masses of the Russian people are as law-abiding as the English. More so, perhaps, because the traditional self-control developed by the long exercise of communal self-government is doubled with them by traditional endurance and submissiveness. Our country seemed destined by nature to follow the English way of reform from above through the action of established authority. But under Alexander II. autocracy has forfeited the chance of taking the lead in such peaceful and uninterrupted progress.

With every new reign it becomes more and more evident that Russia will follow the same road as the rest of continental nations, passing through alternate periods of revolution followed by reaction, which undo most of what has been done before, and thus prepare the ground for a new revolution. A painful and slow process, most disadvantageous from the point of view of economy of strength, but the only one which is imposed upon the continental nations by the fact that their ruling classes, official and middle class alike, have never been able to master the art of their English *confrères* of yielding in time.

The years 1879-82 present us the highest point attained by the revolutionary tide, which made autocracy totter on its foundation. During the years 1887-90 the revolution was at its lowest ebb. But all this while the restless cynicism of the reaction was working unceasingly for a new revolutionary revival, and will not stop hammering on until it succeeds in bringing it about.

What form this revival will take it is impossible to foresee. Imagine three horses running the same race. The black horse of popular insurrections, the red horse of terrorism, and the white horse of military risings. All the three have scoured at different times the vast Russian plains. All the three are undoubtedly in the field now. Which will reach the goal first? The one that will be spurred hardest, that is all one can tell. But which it will be the future alone can show.

The Russian peasants are one of the most patient races on earth; but there was one thing which made them rise in violent rebellion—serfdom. They rebelled against it in the past, and the numerous servile riots of 1850-55 proved that they were on the point of rebelling once again, when the Tzar, Alexander II., had the wisdom to start his timely reforms, in order to substitute, according to his own words, "a revolution from above for a revolution from below."

Now the most striking fact of our domestic policy is the gradual reinstalment of serfdom in its most salient features. We have seen what strides have been made in that direction during the reign of Alexander III. No doubt is possible that the same line will be followed to the bitter end under Nicholas II. The papers announce two important projects of law which will make this reinslavement almost complete. The Government proposes nothing less than to declare all the land held by the peasants, for which some of them have already paid two-thirds of the value, the inalienable property of the State transforming the redemption money into a permanent tax. This means depriving the peasants of all the economic advantages gained by their emancipation and acquired on the strength of it. To complete the picture, there is the other project, which proposes granting the officials the right of sending defaulting tax-payers to any work they choose for them, and the right to receive the wages due to them in payment of the debt to the State.

The first of these measures is likely to be carried out; the second has been carried out; and one asks oneself, what remains of the peasant's freedom? And the question which comes next is, will the peasants stand it, and for how long?

The present international character of European culture, due to the facilities of intellectual and commercial intercommunication, prevents any country from remaining at a standstill. The interior development of Russia is one of the most striking proofs of this fact. It has gone on in all directions, notwithstanding the stagnation of her political institutions, and although the intellectual changes operating among the peasantry may be less palpable than those of her upper classes, owing to the enormous mass of people to be moved, still they are not on that account the less remarkable. The peasants of to-day are a different race from those of thirty years ago.

The whole of our democratic "intelligenza," or intellectual class, is, and has been, devoting its best energies to the work of the enlightenment of the peasantry.

Upon this we have the record of a most interesting official document, which it would be a pity to ignore. It is a confidential communication from the Minister of the Interior to the Minister of Public Education. Its object was to obtain his co-operation in stamping out a certain class of popular literature. But the incidental statements concerning the new movement to the people are still more interesting than the substance of the document. They bear testimony of work which the Minister of the Interior denounces as a danger to the State, and which has been going on uninterruptedly for more than thirty years, in all sort of ways, and by all kinds of means: through school-books, through direct propaganda work—

which the threat of the most drastic punishments has never been able to stop—and through the everyday intercourse of the peasants with their educated brothers. The germs of new ideas have found their way into the minds of the Russian peasants. They have tasted the forbidden fruit.

Very characteristic is the fact that among the addresses asking for participation of the people in the management of State affairs, the Tzar, Nicholas II., received one from the peasants.

It is the first time in Russia that a peasant community has raised its voice in the name of freedom; but it will not be the last. The new generation, which knew not serfdom, has passed through the village schools—schools which no effort of Government could prevent from being the seminaries of broader ideas and feelings.

The modern peasants feel the ignominy of their position like human beings. The papers have reported a number of cases of suicide and some cases of insanity as a consequence of the corporal punishments inflicted. It is impossible but that the reckless policy of the Government towards the rural classes will call forth a more active and effective form of protest. How soon it will come depends upon the amount of energy the autocracy puts into forcing its growth.

The exact time of a movement of any kind of the huge unorganized masses—like the eruptions of a volcano—cannot be predicted. No sign is given until the moment of the eruption comes. But under certain conditions the movement is sure to come, the only question is one of time.

The two other forms of rebellion which our past history offers to us have depended upon the educated classes, and would seem to be more controllable and foreseeable. But this is a mistake. All forms of revolutionary outburst are manifestations of an organic disease of the body politic, and in so far they do not depend upon man's will or preferences.

There can be no two opinions on the question, whether terrorism or military insurrection is the more desirable in the interests of freedom and the general political education of our country.

But it is as impossible to provoke a military insurrection if the historic condition has not created a favourable ground for it, as it is impossible to prevent an outburst of terrorism, when its time has come. Military risings are possible only when some general idea has acted upon the whole mass of the educated class with such vehemence that even the military class has fallen under its influence.

The Decembrist insurrection was the outcome of the great fermentation of spirit caused by the Napoleonic wars, and the occupation by the Russian troops of some French provinces, which brought the officers and soldiers into immediate contact with free institutions.

We have seen that fifteen years ago we had a very near approach to an insurrectionary attempt similar to that of the Decembrists, owing to the profound effect produced by the terrorist struggle, which had stirred up the whole of the Russian people, and showed the weakness of the Government, and had given the revolutionary party the prestige of irresistible strength. Without some such agitation, due to general causes, the military class, living usually outside politics, cannot be induced to join in considerable numbers the ranks of a revolution. This is clear enough, but terrorism itself, although apparently the work of a handful of people, must have its organic causes.

To a great extent it is the work of the

Government. Exceptional—one may say individual — provocation; unendurable deadly outrage to men's honour and most sacred feelings; this alone renders morally possible, and justifies, in the absence of any other means of redress, the fierce mode of retaliation which was adopted at one time by the Russian revolutionists.

But this personal element does not suffice. The Yakutsk butchery and the unspeakable outrages at Kara exceed the worst that was done by official brutality under Alexander II. Yet no act of terrorism followed them; whilst terrorism began to make headway a few years later, when the memory of these offences was less burning, but when the general exasperation against the brutal *régime* had become ever so much keener. Everything that has a political object must have in it the element of hope, and an attack upon the Government, no matter in what form, will take place when the general state of public opinion promises to make it a serious blow to the system. That is why terrorism can more easily have a revival under Nicholas II. than under Alexander III. His position is weaker, because from the very outset he made himself exceeding unpopular by his quixotic reactionism; because he has shown to the very curb-stones that autocracy means permanent stagnation; because he has dispelled all the monarchical illusions, and given people the alternative of renouncing all hope of a better future for Russia, or of directly attacking the autocracy.

This is one condition in which the germs of terrorism may grow. It is not in a spirit of exultation that we point to such a possibility. The experience of the past has shown us how risky, how difficult, and in reality how slow, is the effect of terrorist methods. They narrow the field of action, restrict the fighting forces to revolutionists only, and make it all a pure game of chance. It is the worst of all methods of revolutionary warfare, and there is only one thing that is worse still—slavish submissiveness, and the absence of any protest. We could not look upon the revival of it otherwise than as a disgrace for Russia.

But fortunately there is a means of avoiding this possibility, and we have a fair hope that it will be taken advantage of. It is for the whole of the Liberal Opposition to avail itself of the weakness of the present Government by broad and general protest, which will compel the autocracy either to yield or to make open war on the whole of Russian society, using against it the same drastic measures of reprisal which have been tried so unsuccessfully against the Nihilists. The campaign has been opened by the demonstration of the Zemstvos. After the Tzar's speech of Jan. 20th every such act has become a crime. But they have not stopped on that account, and we hear of other demonstrations and requests of a similar nature.

Authors, lawyers, printers, have come forward with their requests. The moment is very favourable for such a movement; since the time of the pretorian rule of the eighteenth century Russia has not had a Government commanding so little respect. And this intellectual uprising is not likely to stop at petitioning. Open illegal protest, that is the mode of the day, and it is an important sign of the times that the revolutionary party in Russia has fallen in with it. It is highly desirable that foreign public opinion should be on the side of the opposition in this critical moment.

Speaking to the English people, I should like to point out to them that whatever the apparent advantages of an alliance with the Russian Government, the future belongs to the opposition, and the permanent interests of the civilized world lie in the abolition of autocracy in Russia; for there is no safety or peace for the world as long as the present *régime* stands in our country.

THE END.

LONDON:
PRINTED BY GILBERT AND RIVINGTON, LD.,
ST. JOHN'S HOUSE, CLERKENWELL, E.C.

OCTOBER, 1895.

DOWNEY & CO.'S

LIST OF

New and Forthcoming Books

NEW BOOKS.

Hibernia Pacata; or, The Wars in Ireland during the Reign of Queen Elizabeth.
Edited, and with an Introduction and copious Notes, by STANDISH O'GRADY. 2 vols., medium 8vo., with Portraits (some hitherto unpublished), Maps, &c. [*Shortly*.
A Limited Edition only will be issued.

The Poems of J. Sheridan Le Fanu.
Edited by ALFRED PERCEVAL GRAVES. Crown 8vo. [*Shortly*.

The Life of William Carleton (Author of "Traits and Stories of the Irish Peasantry").
By D. J. O'DONOGHUE. 2 vols., large post 8vo., with Portrait. 21*s*. [*Shortly*.

London Town: Sketches of London Life and Character.
By MARCUS FALL. Crown 8vo. [*Just ready*.

Historic Churches of Paris.
With numerous sketches by B.S LE FANU. [*Shortly*.

Hyde Park from Domesday-Book to Date.
By JOHN ASHTON. With numerous Illustrations.

King Stork and King Log: A Study of Modern Russia.
By STEPNIAK. 2 vols., crown 8vo.

Photography, Artistic and Scientific.
By ROBERT JOHNSON, and A. B. CHATWOOD. With fifty-four Photographic Illustrations. 10*s*. 6*d*.

NEW BOOKS.

Boz-land.

By PERCY FITZGERALD. Crown 8vo. With a Portrait of 'Boz' by G. Cruickshank. 6s.

"A charming volume, forming a guide-book to Dickens' places and people."—*World*.

"Only an enthusiast could have written 'Boz-land,' because only an enthusiast could possess so wide and deep a knowledge of the details of 'Boz's' fiction. There is only one Dickens, and Mr. Fitzgerald is his prophet. That is the impression conveyed by this bright, lively, and agreeable volume."—*Globe*.

A Jorum of "Punch": with some account of those who brewed it.

By ATHOL MAYHEW. Illustrated. Imp. 16mo.

The story of the origin and early history of "Punch," with anecdotes of Douglas Jerrold, W. M. Thackeray, Henry and Horace Mayhew, Mark Lemon, Gilbert à Beckett, Albert Smith, &c.

"Will be read with instruction and amusement by all who are interested in the history of journalism."—*Scotsman*.

Russia under the Tzars.

By STEPNIAK. New and Cheaper Edition. Crown 8vo. 2s. 6d.

"Vivid and absorbing."—*Daily Telegraph*.
"Excessively interesting."—*The Times*.

Reminiscences of an old Bohemian.

By G. L. M. STRAUSS. A New and Revised Edition. Crown 8vo. With a Portrait of the Author. 5s.

"It is most excellent garrulity. Dr. Strauss lived the true *vie de Bohème*."—*Daily Telegraph*.

"Amongst the numerous reprints which are things to welcome with thankfulness is Messrs. Downey's revival of a book which will be even more highly appreciated now than it was on its first appearance.... From his Red days to the chapter of theatrical reminiscences, which is invaluable for the preservation of a very vivid and remarkable epoch in the history of the English stage, the writer holds the reader under a spell."—*World*.

The Irish Novelists' Library.

Crown 8vo, fancy cloth, 2s. 6d. net, per volume.

❖❖❖❖❖❖❖❖❖

"We are glad to welcome a series which promises to give us a shelf-full of stories racy of the Irish soil; and a capital start has without doubt been made with 'O'Donnel.'"—*The Speaker.*

MESSRS. DOWNEY & CO. are now publishing, under the general title of *The Irish Novelists' Library*, a series of reprints of the best novels by the most popular Irish novelists.

Each volume of the series is complete in itself, is prefaced by a Biographical and Critical Memoir, and contains a Portrait of the Author.

The first volumes of the series,

O'DONNEL. By LADY MORGAN,

ORMOND. By MISS EDGEWORTH,

FARDOROUGHA THE MISER. By WILLIAM CARLETON,

RORY O'MORE. By SAMUEL LOVER, are now ready.

Other volumes to follow immediately.

"The thanks of the reading public are undoubtedly due to Messrs. Downey for this the initial volume of a series of reprints of the best novels by the most popular Irish novelists, which they intend to issue under the general title of 'The Irish Novelists' Library.' The list of works to follow this shows that great care and a wide range has been taken in the selection, and, printed on good paper, tastefully bound, each with a portrait of the author—in the case of 'O'Donnel' with a photogravure of Lady Morgan from a drawing by Mr. J. F. O'Hea—and published at a very moderate price, this series will no doubt command a wide popularity."—*European Mail.*

NEW NOVELS.

Price 12s. each.

Jack Westropp: an Autobiography.
2 vols.

"Second only to 'Barry Lyndon' as a *tour de force* of audacious satirical and cynical humour."—*The World.*

The Co-Respondent.
By G. W. APPLETON. 2 vols. Second Edition.

"Any one who experiences a craving to indulge in immoderate and uncontrollable laughter can gain immediate satisfaction by perusing Mr. G. W. Appleton's new two-volume novel. It is indisputably one of the funniest stories of the year, full of subtle devices and ingenious contrivances, and positively bristling with comic 'situations.' . . . The fun is not only 'fast and furious,' but unflagging and spontaneous. There should be no limits to the popularity of so brilliantly entertaining a work."—*Daily Telegraph.*

A Dark Intruder.
By RICHARD DOWLING. 2 vols.

"A very ingeniously-constructed mystery plot."—*Saturday Review.*

"An exciting story of modern life . . . the style is bright and rapid."—*Academy.*

"As weird as the imaginings of Edgar Allan Poe."—*Court Journal.*

"A prize sensational story."—*Daily Telegraph.*

"'A Dark Intruder' is nearly as good as 'Gaboriau,' and this is saying much."—*Spectator.*

"Mr. Dowling is the king of sensational story-tellers."—*Lady's Pictorial.*

NEW NOVELS—*continued.*

Price 6s.

A Fallen Star: a Story of the Scots in Prussia.
By CHARLES LOWE. Illustrated by G. Paterson.
[*In the press.*

Ulrick the Ready: a Romance of Elizabethan Ireland. By STANDISH O'GRADY. [*In the press.*

Schoolboys Three. By W. P. KELLY.

The Co-Respondent. By G. W. APPLETON. Fourth Edition.

A Generation. By R. S. SIEVIER. Second Edition.
"I read his book through, and laid it down with the impression that there was real stuff in it of the right sort."—*Westminster Gazette.*

The Adventures of a Ship's Doctor. By MORLEY ROBERTS. With a Frontispiece by A. D. McCormick.
"Told with infinite spirit and much rather grim humour."—*Pall Mall Gazette.*

An Experiment in Respectability. By JULIAN STERN.
"A terrible realistic story."—*Society.*

Golden Lads and Girls. By H. A. HINKSON.
"There is not a page which does not reveal the scholar and the thinker, the sane and reasonable lover of his country, the humorist, and the man who has a reverence for womanhood."—*The World.*

Scholar's Mate. By VIOLET MAGEE.
"The book is written throughout in a humorous vein; its tone is lightly and spontaneously ironical; it bristles with pointed epigrams and brilliant up-to-date notions."—*Daily Telegraph.*

NEW NOVELS—continued.

Price 6s.

The Degradation of Geoffrey Alwith.
By MORLEY ROBERTS.

"An undeniably powerful novel."—*World.*

"Bold in conception and powerful in treatment."—*Scotsman.*

"A brilliant study of one of the most tragic conditions of human life conceivable. . . . Distinctly a book to read—indeed a book to buy—and its power and pathetic realism are irresistible. . . . The book is not only fascinating, but convincing."
Court Journal.

"A strong, painful, and artistic story."—*Illustrated London News.*

"Extremely powerful, artistic, and dramatic."—*Academy.*

Worst Woman in London, and other Stories.
By F. C. PHILIPS.

"Light-hearted, easy-going, and thoroughly readable from end to end."—*Standard.*

"Humour and tenderness, comedy, farce, and tragedy jostle each other in these pages. . . . Mr. Philips writes like a man of the world who has yet contrived to keep a kindly disposition towards its faults and follies."—*Court Journal.*

The Merchant of Killogue.
By F. M. ALLEN.

"Every character in the book is put down in words so subtle and strong that for yourself you know the people. It is an exciting story, with a thrilling winding-up."—*Vanity Fair.*

"An inside and intimate picture of Irish life and character in phases and circumstances which have not, so far as we know, been approached by any other novelist or satirist."—*World.*

The Mahatma: a Tale of Modern Theosophy.

"'The Mahatma' deals with what may be called the witchcraft of to-day. It shows a good deal of grim imagination in its narration of mystic adventures."—*Realm.*

NEW NOVELS—*continued.*

J. SHERIDAN LE FANU'S STORIES.

Torlogh O'Brien: a Story of the Wars
of King James. Illustrated by Phiz. [*Shortly.*

A Chronicle of Golden Friars, and other
Stories. Illustrated by B. S. LE FANU and J. F. O'HEA. 5s. [*Shortly.*

The Cock and Anchor.
Illustrated by B. S. LE FANU. 5s.

"Full of incident and adventure."—*Leeds Mercury.*

The Evil Guest.
Illustrated by B. S. LE FANU. 5s.

"It shows throughout a concentrated power which renders it one of the most characteristic of the author's works. No more excellent interpreter of his father's text could be desired than Mr. Brinsley Le Fanu, whose quaint old-world illustrations harmonise perfectly with the tone of the book."—*Morning Post.*

The Watcher, and other Weird Stories.
Illustrated by B. S. LE FANU. 3s. 6d. net.

"The stories, one and all, bear the marks of Mr. Le Fanu's peculiar genius."—*Pall Mall Gazette.*

"The editor's selection is entirely successful, and his illustrations of the book prove his possession, *par droit de naissance,* of skill, feeling, and taste."—*World.*

NEW NOVELS—continued.

Price 3s. 6d.

Shadows on Love's Dial. By the QUEEN OF ROUMANIA. [*Just ready.*

The Ragged Edge : Stories of the African
Gold-fields. By ANNA, COMTESSE DE BREMONT.

"Bright and interesting."—*Scotsman.*

Princess and Priest. A. S. F. HARDY.
With a Preface by Professor SAYCE.

" If it were only for the sake of the descriptions of Egyptian life, of the mystic ceremonies, and the beliefs of the priests, the book would be worth reading; but as it includes an entertaining story as well, it becomes a volume to be in every way recommended."—*Daily Telegraph.*

Mrs. Bouverie. By F. C. PHILIPS.

"'Mrs. Bouverie' is delightful."—*Standard.*
"Certainly this is a book to read—more than once."—*Vanity Fair.*

Starlight through the Roof. By KEVIN KENNEDY.

"The author is an artist. He has made his characters live and speak."—*Saturday Review.*

Ballybeg Junction. By F. M. ALLEN.
Illustrated by JOHN F. O'HEA.

" Genuine uproarious fun."—*Academy.*
" Mr. Allen's high spirits never flag."—*Athenæum.*
" As funny as anything given us by Charles Lever."—*Star.*

NEW NOVELS—continued.

Price 3s. 6d.

Brayhard: the Strange Adventures of One Ass and Seven Champions. By F. M. ALLEN. With 37 Illustrations by HARRY FURNISS.

"Those who have read and laughed at 'Through Green Glasses' and 'The Voyage of the Ark' will enjoy Mr. Allen's new book, for it has all his own peculiar humour, and is brimful of jokes, repartees, and comic situations, which seem to run off the author's pen as naturally as does the ink."—*Guardian.*

Anchor-Watch Yarns. By EDMUND DOWNEY. Illustrated by M. FITZGERALD.

"His sailors are true to life, and evidently studied from living models. . . . There is manifested throughout a keen sense of humour."—*Morning Post.*

Captain Lanagan's Log. By EDMUND DOWNEY. Illustrated by MATT STRETCH.

"A rattling volume of sea adventure."—*Melbourne Argus.*
"The book is full of excitement and fun."—*Glasgow Herald.*

The Land Smeller. By EDMUND DOWNEY.

"It is a joy to come across such a work."—*Pall Mall Gazette.*
"Mr. Downey has the power of being humorous in a simple, genuine fashion, without the least vulgarity."—*Athenæum.*
"Uncommonly bracing reading."—*Scotsman.*

In One Town. By EDMUND DOWNEY. With a Frontispiece by GORDON BROWNE.

"Quite out of the ordinary run of novels. . . . The whole atmosphere of the book is redolent of the sea. . . A story of unusual merit, by turns romantic, pathetic and humorous."—*Westminster Review.*

NEW NOVELS—*continued.*

Price 2s. 6d.

A Sensational Trance. By FORBES DAWSON. Illustrated by F. MACKENZIE.

"A purely fantastic vein has never more thoroughly been worked out than in Mr. Dawson's story."—*Scotsman.*

"Mr. Forbes Dawson has a truly remarkable imagination."—*Star.*

"The story is told with a breezy straightforwardness which is exhilarating."—*Pelican.*

Through Green Glasses. By F. M. ALLEN. A new Edition. Illustrated by M. Fitzgerald. 23rd Thousand.

A House of Tears. By EDMUND DOWNEY. A new Edition. With a Frontispiece by Gordon Browne. 20th Thousand.

[*In the Press.*

DOWNEY & CO., Publishers,
12, YORK ST., COVENT GARDEN, LONDON, W.C.

www.ingramcontent.com/pod-product-compliance
Lightning Source LLC
Chambersburg PA
CBHW031829230426
43669CB00009B/1275